The Essential Elias Hicks

Paul Buckley

Inner Light Books
San Francisco, California

The Essential Elias Hicks

Cover and book design: Paul Buckley

Front cover painting used by permission of Percy Hicks Severn

Rear cover photograph by Patricia Jane Pennell, Riverhouse Photography

Published by Inner Light Books, San Francisco, California

www.innerlightbooks.com

editor@innerlightbooks.com

Library of Congress Control Number: 2013949617

ISBN 978-0-9834980-8-7 (hardcover)

ISBN 978-0-9834980-9-4 (paperback)

"For if thou willingly surrenders thyself as an offering to God – to do his will, as by the Light in thy own heart and conscience he is pleased to manifest it to thee – thy understanding will be more and more opened into those things that concern thy present and everlasting peace."

(Letters, p. 77)

Dedicated to John Punshon

for his encouragement & example.

Table of Contents

Introduction

"Flee, O my soul, to thy rock, the name of the Lord! For in it is safety and a sure refuge from all the storms and tempests that assail poor mortals in passing through this vale of tears and state of trial and probation."
(Journal, p. 145)

In April 1827, the Religious Society of Friends suffered a rupture of a magnitude it had never endured in its previous one hundred and seventy five years. A minor procedural dispute in Philadelphia Yearly Meeting[1] brought a deep and long-running fault-line to the surface. In the end, a majority of the yearly meeting's members withdrew and formed a new organization which they claimed was the true Philadelphia Yearly Meeting. Those left behind carried on, also claiming to be Philadelphia Yearly Meeting. Over the next year, the separation spread to the Yearly Meetings of New York, Baltimore, Ohio, and Indiana, producing a total of five parallel yearly meetings. The splits propagated down through subordinate quarterly meetings, monthly meetings, and preparative meetings, opening a fissure that has never healed.

Very soon, each faction declared those in the other party were no longer Friends. One side claimed it followed orthodox Quaker principles, while their opponents were "Hicksites" - followers of Elias Hicks, a minister from a small meeting on Long Island. In the same way, the "Hicksites" maintained they were the only true Quakers, and branded their opponents as "the Orthodox."

Because of those separations, the name Elias Hicks has acquired a multitude of associations among Friends. Many assume Hicksites came by their name because Hicks encouraged the separations and the establishment of a new sect. This was not the case.

---

[1] A description of the structure, practices, and some of the terminology of the Religious Society of Friends (Quakers) in the early nineteenth century is presented in an appendix.

Over the last two centuries, the branches of the Society of Friends have evolved in very different directions. Descendants of the Hicksites are often labeled as "liberal Quakers." It seems reasonable, therefore, to assume Hicks must have been a liberal and the most recent biography of Hicks[2] labels him as one. This is also an error.

A variety of beliefs were attributed to him during his lifetime and even more have been since his death. Since Elias Hicks never attempted to delineate his beliefs in a systematic way, there has been no standard against which to judge the conflicting claims. Nor has an organized record of his theology been published in the years since he died.

The purpose of this book is to discover the true Elias Hicks and to lay out his beliefs in an orderly manner. The first chapter is a brief biography and the succeeding chapters are devoted to topics of importance in his life.

This book aims to be more than just an interpretation of who Elias Hicks was and what he believed. It is almost a dialogue between Hicks and the author. In the text, the two voices are distinguished by the typography. My descriptions of Hicks and his beliefs will be printed in standard type, while quotes from Hicks will be indented and in italic.

The Religious Society of Friends

Elias Hicks was a Quaker. This was part of his core identity and to understand him, some knowledge of the Religious Society of Friends is essential - both what it looked like when he was born and how it changed over the course of his lifetime.

Quakerism emerged in the immediate aftermath of the English civil wars. George Fox, credited as the founder of the movement, had a vision while on top of Pendle Hill in northwest England on Pentecost Sunday in 1652. He reported he was given to see, "A great people to be gathered." This vision inspired him to travel throughout England, Ireland, Scotland, Wales, Holland, Germany, and the British colonies in the West Indies and North America, preaching, "Christ Jesus has come to teach his people himself."

Inward Light

Central to the Quaker message is the belief that each person has direct access to the mind of God by the medium of the "Inward Light of Christ."

---

[2] Bliss Forbush, *Elias Hicks: Quaker Liberal*, New York: Columbia University Press, 1956.

According to Friends, this Light is described in John 1:9: "That was the true Light, which lighteth every man that cometh into the world."[3]

Friends claim this "Light Within" originates in the divine and illuminates each person's heart and soul. It provides knowledge of good and evil, letting people know when they fail to live up to the hopes and desires God has for them, but it does more than just to admonish. This Inward Teacher also provides unfailing guidance for life. Those who faithfully listen to it and submit to its direction have all that is needed for salvation. Moreover, this Divine Light is universally available. Everyone has equal access, not just Quakers or Christians. It can guide anyone - even those who practice no religion - to reconciliation with God, if they heed its proddings.

During the second half of the seventeenth century, Friends endured repeated waves of persecution. Between 1652 and 1689, thousands of Quakers were imprisoned and hundreds died for their faith. But the fires of oppression didn't destroy the society; they only strengthened the resolve of the persecuted.

Quaker Peculiarities & Worship

During this period, Friends developed a number of distinguishing characteristics. Prescribed uniforms evolved - simple, unadorned, white, gray, and black "plain clothes." Friends also came to speak in a distinctive manner. At the time, it was considered polite to address those in a higher social class with the second person plural forms - "you" and "your." Quakers, however, used the second person singular - "thee," "thou," and "thy" - when speaking to single individuals of all classes. Despite being persecuted, Quakers acted in ways that made them stand out.

Based on instructions in the Bible, they refused to swear oaths - even in court. They said they were compelled to be truthful all the time, not just when under oath. They claimed they could not participate in any act of war. They declared the outward rites and rituals practiced by other Christians, such as baptizing with water and celebrating the supper with bread and wine, were no longer needed. Already in trouble with the government, they broke the law by refusing to pay tithes to the established church. They said they were the only true Christians.

---

[3] Bible quotations are from the King James Version.

These Quakers gathered to worship in a simple building they called a meetinghouse, not a church. Coming together with no preplanned order of service, no scripture readings or sermons, and with no worship leader, the congregation gathered in silence at a designated time. If one or more members felt called by God to preach or teach or sing, they would do so. It was assumed anyone present could be divinely inspired to minister - even women, children, and servants. Although women and men sat on opposite sides of the meetinghouse, there was no barrier between them during worship and any ministry offered was heard by all.

Unlike other banned sects, Friends held their meetings for worship openly - in their meetinghouses and at their usual times. This blatant violation of the law infuriated some in the established church, resulting in services being broken up by mass arrests and the destruction of their meetinghouses. They were troublesome and unbending in their demands for religious freedom.

Toleration

Everything changed following the "Glorious Revolution" of 1688 in England. The next year, Parliament passed the Act of Toleration. With this change in law, most Protestants were free to hold worship services without government interference. There were still restrictions on Friends (e.g., they could not enroll in universities and were excluded from certain professions), but life became much easier.

Over the next sixty years, two major changes took place. In their private lives, Quietism, the belief people need to entirely quiet the inner voice of their own wills in order to hear the voice of God, became entrenched in Quaker spiritual practice. Any impulse that originated within the individual was suspect.

During the same years, members of the religious society increasingly accommodated themselves to the wider world in their public lives. Those unique characteristics that set them apart from the rest of the world were de-emphasized. Rather than seeing themselves as a people called out of the world to be "a Light unto the Gentiles," the society seemed more and more to be just another Protestant sect. Unlike their forbearers, by the middle of the eighteenth century, most Quakers no longer claimed to be the only true Christians - the Religious Society of Friends was merely one part of a larger body of Christ.

A Quaker Reformation

In the middle of the eighteenth century, a reformation movement swept through Quakerism.[4] The reformers saw accommodation to the world as a slow poison. As the religious society gradually adopted the world's ways of doing and being, they believed it was becoming less able to fulfill the unique role God had called Friends to fill. These reformers felt a need to purify the society and for Friends to more closely adhere to traditional practices. This was not principally a call for doctrinal purity, but for behavioral conformity. Most disownments were for such things as public drunkenness and marriage to non-Friends.[5] In the eyes of the reformers, this cleansed the society - no doubt reducing it in size, but forging it into a faithful remnant.

Overseers

One development coincident with the reformation (if not a product of it) was the establishment and spread of the office of Overseer. While Ministers preached and Elders concerned themselves with the spiritual state of the society, Overseers watched over outward behavior.

In principle, the job of the Overseer was to intervene with wayward members before their behavior became too public - helping, counseling, and encouraging them to find a way back to their proper places within the society. A successful intervention avoided embarrassment for the member and obviated the need for public discipline or disownment by the meeting. Danger arose when the scope of intervention moved beyond concern for outward behavior to include a consideration of a member's faith. There had been a relatively broad range of acceptable beliefs during the society's first hundred years, but as it moved toward the beginning of the nineteenth century, some among the leadership began to feel more doctrinal uniformity was necessary.

---

[4] For a full description of this movement, see Jack D. Marietta, *The Reformation of American Quakerism, 1748-1783*, Philadelphia: University of Pennsylvania Press, 1989

[5] Marietta reports there were nearly thirteen thousand cases of discipline brought to Friends meetings in Philadelphia Yearly Meeting in the century between its founding and the end of the American Revolution. Of these, a mere fifteen involved theological concerns and resulted in only three disownments. There were nearly five thousand incidents concerning marriage and a bit more than two thousand involving fornication – mostly instances of premarital sex between engaged couples.

Changes in the Wider World

Both the Religious Society of Friends and the wider world passed through dramatic transitions during Elias Hicks' lifetime. What he believed and how he conducted his life are to a great degree products of his Quaker milieu, but he was also unavoidably influenced by the many changes in the wider world.

When Elias Hicks was born in 1748, he was a colonial subject of George II, King of Great Britain and an empire that included provinces in North America. These provinces were thinly stretched along the Atlantic coast - barely extending into the continent as far as the crest of the Appalachian Mountains. There were one million colonists with the overwhelming majority living on small farms. No urban area in the colonies had a population greater than twenty-five thousand.

By the time Elias Hicks died in 1830, he lived among more than twelve million citizens of the United States - a republic claiming territory that extended across the continent to the Pacific Ocean. Most of these citizens still lived on farms, but the growth of cities was well underway - New York City alone contained over two hundred thousand inhabitants.

These were revolutionary times in many ways besides the American and French Revolutions. Catherine the Great and Napoleon re-arranged the map of Europe. The Enlightenment spurred an ongoing scientific revolution. That, in turn, helped fuel an industrial revolution. It was an era of scientific discoveries and new ideas - Goethe, Voltaire, Mary Wollstonecraft, James Watt, Linnaeus, Samuel Johnson, Adam Smith, Jane Austen, Beethoven, and Mozart are only a few of those who were transforming science, philosophy, and the arts. The modern world was starting to take shape.

More important to the future of the Society of Friends, were the revolutionary changes in the sphere of religion. In the first half of the eighteenth century, George Whitefield had helped spark the First Great Awakening in England's American colonies and paved the way for future waves of religious revival.

In the middle of the century, the preaching of John and Charles Wesley led to the creation of the Methodist Church. When Hicks was born, there were no Methodists - when he died, there were more Methodist Churches in the United States than post offices. Wesleyan theology offered a sure path to salvation by the guidance of scripture and laid the foundations for evangelical Protestantism.

Women were also playing a more prominent role in religious life. Mother Ann Lee set up the first community of Shakers in 1779; while in 1809, Mother Elizabeth Ann Seton established the Catholic Sisters of Charity to work in the new urban slums. In a harbinger of important future work for Quakers, 1816 marked Elizabeth Gurney Fry's first visit with women imprisoned in London's Newgate Prison.

The World's Influence on Friends

Eighteenth-century Friends still wore distinctive clothing, spoke their unique and somewhat archaic form of English, maintained their own schools, and expected members only to marry other members. Many lived in distinct urban neighborhoods or rural communities, thus spending most of their time with others in the faith. But it would have been impossible to live through those years without being aware of the dramatic changes taking place in the wider culture. Hicks preferred to ignore these changes and wished other Quakers would, too. Rather than joining in the "spirit, manners, maxims, and customs" of the wider world, he advocated that Friends maintain a "hedge" around the society, separating and protecting those within from outside influences. Like many Friends before and since, he saw Quakerism as a critique of and an alternative to the surrounding culture. Hicks was sure God was still calling Quakers out of the world to be a light unto the Gentiles.

Holes in the Hedge

But the hedge was incomplete and full of holes; Quakers constantly absorbed new ideas from their neighbors. Religiously, some were influenced by Deists and Unitarians. These Friends also tended to be open to Rationalism - the belief religious faith should be based on human reason. Other Friends were won over to the evangelical theology championed by John and Charles Wesley and had powered successive waves of spiritual awakening throughout British North America and the United States. In contrast to rationalism - and to the Quietism that prevailed among Friends - revivalists sought an emotional response from their congregations. Grafting any of these concepts into Quakerism had enormous implications for the role of the Inward Light and proper forms of worship. As these hybrids took root, they inevitably exacerbated preexisting conflicts within the society that ultimately gave birth to separations in 1827-28.

Intentionally or not, Elias Hicks was at the heart of those conflicts. His preaching - especially in public meetings for non-Quakers - was a lightning rod, attracting the ire of some Friends, especially those who found truth in evangelical thought. What they heard him say was, to their ears, grievously in error. Knowing what kinds of unsoundness he was charged with - as contrasted to what he actually believed - offers essential insight into some of the most tragic events in Quaker history.

Things I Believe But Can't Prove

I have been living with Elias Hicks for well over a decade and have come to believe some things that go beyond what I can demonstrate in the paper trail he or others left behind. My personal inclination is to keep my opinions to myself, but my wife insists readers will want to know what insights these years of close study have yielded. To accommodate her without misleading readers, some of the chapters below will include subsections with the title "Things I Believe But Can't Prove." Take them with a grain of salt.

Changes in the Religious Society of Friends

For example, I believe there were three large-scale shocks to the Religious Society of Friends over the course of Elias Hicks' lifetime that dramatically changed it and helped to set the stage for the Great Separations of 1827-28.

Unintended Consequences of Reformation

The first was the reformation of the society in the middle of the eighteenth century, mentioned above. Stricter enforcement of the discipline resulted in many more disownments in the years after 1750 than in the first half of the century. The resulting religious community was smaller and more homogeneous, but disownments also meant more members were related to, and lived in close proximity to, non-members.

It should be noted that movement was not exclusively out of the religious society. Converts were still attracted, perhaps in part because the reformed society had a clear, consistent view of how to live a faithful life. Several important evangelical Friends were convinced in these years; David Sands had been brought up as a Long Island Presbyterian, Stephen

Grellet was a Jansenist Catholic before fleeing revolutionary France, and Thomas Shillitoe, an Anglican in England. On the other side of the divide, William B. Irish joined Friends after exchanging letters with Elias Hicks.

Converts have characteristics that may have contributed to a combative atmosphere. They may unconsciously carry beliefs and attitudes of their religious upbringing with them - often identifying those beliefs as being essentially Quaker. Also significant to the society they joined, they tend to be more zealous than the average birthright member.

Revolutionary Side Effects

A second jolt to Quakerism was the American Revolution. The Religious Society of Friends was formally neutral which meant its members were distrusted by both sides. Patriots suspected them of being loyalists, and Tories, of secretly supporting the rebellion. Living faithfully between the camps - sometimes literally - was a constant challenge.

Relatively large numbers of Quaker men served in the armies - mostly on the American side - and were consequently disowned. Other Quaker men and women actively supported the revolution without directly taking up arms. For example, a substantial number of Friends in Philadelphia withdrew from the yearly meeting and built their own meetinghouse. This "Free Quaker" congregation (which included Betsy Ross) lasted until 1836. A result of these disownments and withdrawals was that Quaker communities, both rural villages and urban neighborhoods, encompassed ever more non-Friends.

Difficulties in mixing with the wider society were compounded at the end of the war, when many Tories fled or were forcibly expelled from the new republic. Because Friends were unwilling for religious reasons to swear an oath of allegiance to the new government, they were vulnerable to the charge of being British loyalists. Some Quakers were driven out of their homes based solely on the accusation of a jealous neighbor or business rival. Exiles were frequently banished on very short notice, leaving little or no time to sell a farm or business. They were often forbidden to take more than personal items with them. State governments seized the "abandoned" property and sold it to pay off war debts.

Internal Migration

The society was further unsettled when the new federal government opened vast new lands for settlement. In 1763, the British government had reserved all lands beyond the crest of the Appalachian Mountains for the exclusive use of the Native Americans. The United States government opened this territory up to settlers and many Quakers were among the migrants. In some cases, whole Quaker communities moved together – notably those removing from Georgia and the Carolinas to Indiana and Ohio to distance themselves from slavery. More often, single individuals and families would emigrate, opening new "holes" in the communities left behind – homes and businesses often filled by non-Quakers.

Friends who had previously lived, worked, and shopped, for the most part, with other Friends now found themselves more frequently in direct contact with "the people of the world." As a result, the hedge was further weakened and increasingly they encountered, thought about, and assimilated the new ideas they were exposed to. The influx of these ideas helped prepare the ground for the coming separations.

Reformation, revolution, and migration were hammer blows to a way of life. To survive, the Society of Friends needed either to retreat and resist – as the Amish did – or to adapt.

In his heart, Elias Hicks denied the changes were inevitable. He worked mightily to maintain the society of his youth, although even he unconsciously incorporated new ideas into that vision. His vocal and public resistance to change was welcomed by some, but in the end, rejected by most – Hicksite and Orthodox alike. Changes came and with them, schism.

Challenges

Elias Hicks lived in very different times and it is tempting to treat him as merely an historic figure – someone who lived a long time ago who has little to say to Friends today. I have found him to be a thoughtful and careful thinker, who tries to apply Friends' fundamental principles to the issues he encounters. Sometimes, that leads him to conclusions very different from those espoused by most twenty-first-century Friends. I have found his ideas worth engaging – even when I don't agree.

At the end of some of chapters, where I find his thinking particularly provocative or stimulating, I will try to summarize it and form it into one or more queries for the reader's consideration.

Sources

This book depends primarily on two sources: *The Journal of Elias Hicks*[1] (*Journal*) and *Dear Friend: Letters and Essays of Elias Hicks*[2] (*Letters*). Since the journal, letters, and a few essays are the only written materials Hicks produced, they are the best sources available to explore Hicks' beliefs, values, and attitudes. These are both new editions of works first published after his death. A version of the journal was published in 1832[3] and a collection of letters in 1834.[4] Both of these volumes were heavily edited by a committee of the Hicksite New York Yearly Meeting. Apparently motivated by a desire to protect both Hicks and the Hicksites from potential embarrassment, all dreams and visions and most of Hicks' considerations of spiritual or doctrinal matters - constituting about one-quarter of the original manuscripts - were eliminated from the printed texts. This material has been restored in the new editions.

The journal is better described as a memoir. Hicks compiled it in the last year of his life and it provides detailed descriptions of his travels and his life at home. All-in-all, it is a revealing portrait of his principles in practice.

His letters and essays contain a wealth of information on his beliefs, although not laid out in a systematic form. Of particular value are the letters between Hicks and William Poole, Jr. of Wilmington, Delaware. Between 1817 and 1828, Hicks and Poole exchanged at least one hundred thirty-seven letters.[5] These are, in essence, an extended conversation between two thoughtful and perceptive Quakers, observing, involved in, and greatly concerned about the events leading up to the most important schism in the history of the Religious Society of Friends.

---

[1] Buckley, Paul (Ed.), *The Journal of Elias Hicks*, San Francisco: Inner Light Books, 2009.

[2] Buckley, Paul (Ed.), *Dear Friend Letters and Essays of Elias Hicks*, San Francisco: Inner Light Books, 2011.

[3] Hicks, Elias, *Journal of the Life and Religious Labours of Elias Hicks*, New York: Isaac T. Hopper, 1832.

[4] Hicks, Elias, *Letters of Elias Hicks, Including Also a Few Short Essays Written on Several Occasions, Mostly Illustrative of His Doctrinal Views*, New York: Published by Isaac Hopper, 1834.

[5] Buckley, Paul (Ed.), *Thy Affectionate Friend: The Letters of Elias Hicks & William Poole*, Richmond, IN: Earlham School of Religion, unpublished Master's Thesis, 2001.

In addition to these primary sources, three secondary sources have provided useful. Of greatest value was *Quakers in Conflict,* Larry Ingle's masterful history of the Hicksite/Orthodox separation in Philadelphia Yearly Meeting.[6] Two somewhat dated biographies were also referenced. *The Life and Labors of Elias Hicks* by Henry W. Wilbur[7] was published in 1910 and depended on the 1830s editions of the journal and a collection of letters. A more recent biography appeared in 1956.[8] In writing it, Bliss Forbush made use of many of the original manuscripts now in the Friends Historical Library collection at Swarthmore College, but an underlying bias is revealed in his title, *Elias Hicks: Quaker Liberal.* Elias Hicks was not a liberal.

Finally, although many Friends have found great value in the transcripts of some of Elias Hicks vocal ministry, these have not been used directly in the preparation of this text. Several volumes of "Quaker sermons" were published in the 1820s. Hicks was one of the Friends whose preaching was taken down during public meetings and printed – without approval of either the individuals or the yearly meetings. These allow a glimpse of Hicks as an orator, but likely suffer from the same deficiencies as the 1830s editions of his journal and letters.

Friends' universal practice at that time was to offer vocal ministry without notes or other advance preparation. As a result, there are no manuscripts against which to judge the accuracy of these publications. Furthermore, editorial standards in the 1820s permitted far more modification than is currently practiced. Misunderstood or altered words or phrases cannot be identified and corrected. If a section was omitted entirely, it is lost forever.

Admittedly, the published sermons probably have had nothing added to what was said at the time. They appear to contain nothing that directly contradicts or significantly adds to what Hicks wrote in his letters or journal, but there is no way to know what, if any, changes have been made. For these reasons, they were not used in preparing this book.

---

[6] Ingle, H. Larry, *Quakers in Conflict: The Hicksite Reformation*, Wallingford, PA: Pendle Hill, 1998.

[7] Henry W. Wilbur, *The Life and Labors of Elias Hicks*, Philadelphia: Published by Friends General Conference Advancement Committee, 1910.

[8] Bliss Forbush, *Elias Hicks: Quaker Liberal*, New York: Columbia University Press, 1956.

Acknowledgements

This book is the culmination of fifteen years of work and there are so many people who have contributed to it, I hardly know where to start. First, I owe more than you can imagine to my wife, Peggy Spohr, who has accepted my mania for all that time. She recognized the importance of the book's title. Each time I wanted to add more material, she would gently ask, "Is that *essential*?" Readers owe her an enormous debt of gratitude for keeping me on track.

Next, Charles Martin, the Inner Light Books publisher, has been unstinting in his encouragement for the whole three book project. When I was stuck and unsure how to proceed, Charles read perfectly awful early drafts and somehow found something of value in them. Elizabeth Yeats, the Inner Light Copy Editor, made invaluable comments and suggestions.

The unpublished manuscripts of Elias Hicks' memoirs, essays, and letters in the Friends Historical Library of Swarthmore College provided the raw materials from which the preceding two books were crafted and thus, are the foundation for this book. The library staff, especially Christopher Densmore, Patricia O'Donnell, Susanna W. Morikawa, and Mary Ellen Chijioke (now University Librarian at Godfrey Okoye University in Enugu, Nigeria) was exceptionally helpful and gracious.

Many members of the Richmond, Indiana Quaker community were valuable advisors. Mary Garman, Thomas Hamm, Stephen Angell, and Paul Kriese come immediately to mind. There are so many others.

I have been blessed with several other capable reviewers. H. Larry Ingle read and made greatly appreciated comments on early drafts of several chapters. When I wanted a non-Quaker review, I have asked my mother, Mildred Buckley. She noticed when I was slipping into Quaker jargon and asked for important clarifications at several places in the text.

The photograph on the back cover was taken by Patricia Jane Pennell, Riverhouse Photography.

Finally, Percy Hicks Severn, a descendant of Elias Hicks, has provided consistent encouragement as this project has unfolded. She is also the owner of the oil painting reproduced on the cover of this book. It appears with her permission.

The Essential Biography

"O time, precious time! How swift thou passes on by us, almost unenjoyed and unimproved. How soon thou wilt land thy traveling pilgrim in the house appointed for all living, where, O my soul, thou knows there is no repentance nor amendment known. Prepare then. O prepare for thy bed of clay."
(Journal, p. 185)

Why would an eighty-year-old man choose to travel from Long Island, New York to Richmond, Indiana in 1828? He drove an open, horse-drawn carriage over poor roads and, in some places, no roads - across the spine of the Appalachian Mountains and into the harshness of winter. What compelled Elias Hicks to undertake such foolishness?

By that age, he had survived several heart attacks, frequent and painful kidney stones, chronic pain from arthritis, an extended episode of sciatica, and frequent "touches of bodily indisposition." He was old, tired, and worn. Hicks had already traveled many thousands of miles in faithful service to the Religious Society of Friends and had earned a peaceful retirement, but instead, he set out on the longest journey of his life.

Since his marriage fifty-seven years earlier, he had supported himself and his family as a farmer, but his true vocation had been as a traveling minister. Scores of times in the previous half-century, he had felt God calling him to "perform a religious visit to Friends and others." That spring, he sensed the divine call was renewed:

"Having felt an exercise and travail of spirit in the course of the last year, to pay a religious visit in the love of the gospel to Friends and others in some parts of our own yearly meeting and in the compass of the yearly meetings of Philadelphia, Baltimore, Ohio, Indiana, and a few meetings in Virginia - and apprehending the time had come to move therein - I spread the concern before my Friends at Jericho Monthly Meeting held the 20th of 3rd

month 1828,[1] and obtained their unity and concurrence, certified in their certificate, and signed by the clerks of the men's and women's meetings. Which concern, with the certificate from our monthly meeting, I laid before our quarterly meeting held at Westbury, the 24th of 4th month following, and obtained their unity and concurrence, with an endorsement thereof on my certificate signed by the clerk." (Journal, p. 399)

As he had so many times before, he submitted this sense of a divine leading to his Quaker meeting and waited for their discernment before leaving home. This response reveals two standards that guided his life: absolute submission to God's will and unwavering adherence to the practices of the Religious Society of Friends.

His devotion to these principles produced a life of arduous travel, but it also inevitably involved Elias Hicks in the Great Separations of 1827-28 – schisms among American Friends that split Quakerism into two contentious camps and set the direction for the future evolution of the society.

Birth

Elias Hicks was born on his family's farm near Westbury, New York on the 19th day of the 3rd month 1748 (May 30, 1748)[2] and died about five miles away in Jericho, New York on February 27, 1830, but in the course of his lifetime, he traveled far further than most men of his time. He was a birthright member of the Religious Society of Friends, reporting that at the time of his birth his father had recently become a Quaker, although his mother never took membership in any religious body.

A Wild Youth

His memoirs and correspondence tell very little of his early years on Long Island – most notably of a vision he had when he was about seven years old. His mother died when he was about eleven years old and two years later he was sent to live with an older brother for the summer. Being "almost without any restraint," he indulged in "horse races, card playing,

---

[1] Quakers traditionally did not use the common names for the days of the week and months of the year, since some of those names originally honored pagan gods. Instead, these were simply numbered. For example, Thor's Day (Thursday) was called Fifth Day and March, the month dedicated to Mars, the Roman war god, was termed Third Month.

[2] Great Britain and its empire did not adopt the Gregorian calendar until September 14, 1752. Dates before then have been converted to the equivalent modern date.

and other vain amusements." Of that summer, he wrote "I lost much of my youthful innocence and became considerably hardened in sin and vanity" (*Journal*, p. 5). This initiated an undisciplined adolescence. In his journal, he confessed a variety of misbehaviors, including a veiled reference to bundling:

> *"And now arriving to a state of manhood, I was much exposed – more especially in consequence of a very pernicious and hurtful custom that prevailed through the unwarrantable indulgence of parents in this and some other parts of our country, viz, that of young people getting together in companies, more especially on the evenings of the First Days of the week. And after passing the evening until late in foolish and vain conversation and some other vain amusements, then to couple out, as the young men and young women could agree and retire in secret, where they spent the rest of the night, frequently in beds together." (Journal, p. 7)*

Poor choices in his companions offered a convenient, but inadequate excuse for his "running out." Ultimately, he knew his behavior was of his own choosing and, in fact, he often chose well. Solitary periods spent hunting and fishing provided frequent opportunities for quiet reflection. Moreover, he knew he was not alone – the Lord was his constant companion:

> *"I have oft thought, had it not been for the delight I took in my gun and in angling for fish, that occupied most of my leisure hours, I might have run out with my vain companions – with which I was surrounded – into many excesses to my utter ruin. For although the Lord was graciously near to my poor soul, and followed me with his reproofs, and often set my sins in order before me, and brought me under judgment, and his dread made me afraid, yet through the proneness of my natural desires after self-gratification, by giving way thereto, I was often led to exceed the bounds of reason and truth, and thereby commit sin." (Journal, pp. 4-5)*

His wild youth reached its climax on a dance floor when Elias experienced what earlier generations of Friends termed a day of visitation. This was a time about which he reported, "my soul was deeply sensible of its evil and folly… and was struck with a belief that if I now gave way after forming so many resolutions and should again rebel against the Light, I might be left in an obdurate situation and never have another offer of pardon." Some today might say he was born again: "the Lord was graciously near, and as my cry was secretly to him for strength, he enabled me to covenant with him." (*Journal*, pp. 9-10)

Marriage & Children

On January 2, 1771, this covenant with God and the Society of Friends was further sealed when he wed Jemima Seaman. She was to be the outward rock on which his inward journey was founded. At the time of her marriage, Jemima was an only child and her parents invited the young couple to take up residence on the Seaman farm. Six years later, both of Jemima's parents died and the young couple inherited the land. This brought more financial stability than Elias could ever have anticipated. As the fourth of six sons, he had no real hope of inheriting his own family's farm, so he had apprenticed as a carpenter - work that would have provided an adequate income - but a farm offered much better prospects.

Jemima and Elias had eleven children - four sons and seven daughters. The youngest daughter was still-born (not uncommon at the time) and their second daughter died when two years old of small pox (also too common), but of his daughters, he reported "the rest all arrived to years of discretion and afforded us considerable comfort." But his sons died young:

> *"All four of our sons were weakly and never able to take care of themselves, being all taken off their legs so as not to be able to walk after the ninth or tenth year of their age. The two eldest deceased in the fifteenth year of their age, the third about the seventeenth, and the youngest was near nineteen years when he deceased." (Journal, p. 16)*

All four boys probably died from a genetic form of muscular dystrophy inherited from their mother. In this respect, it is notable Jemima had no living brothers, although Long Island records indicate three sons had been born to her parents.[3] Moreover, their first-born grandson, Elias Willets, died of the same disease in 1818. A lethal-recessive gene, passed on the X-chromosome - through the maternal lineage - would not affect a woman, but would be expressed in any man who carried it.

Traveling in the Ministry

Elias Hicks' career as a traveling minister began in 1779. A dispute had arisen within New York Yearly Meeting and a group of Friends was sent to Philadelphia Yearly Meeting for advice on how to settle it. Among those chosen for this journey was young Elias. This was the first of many journeys.

---

[3] http://www.longislandsurnames.com/genealogy

It was nearly two years before he traveled in the ministry again, but this second trip shows his measure as a Quaker. Fighting in the Revolutionary War had created zones of American and British control with nearly-deserted swatches of contested territory in between. Hicks and his companions had to pass through the armies on their way. As known non-combatants, Quakers crossed the lines without incident, but in no-man's-land, Hicks encountered two bandits.

> *"I, being a little ahead of the company, was first met and accosted by them in a very rough manner – I not seeing them until they spake and one of them demanded very roughly where we were going. I looked upon him in a very mild manner and informed where we intended – without the least interruption of mind. He then interrogated me further as to where we had been, what was our business, and where we were from, etc. To all which, I gave true and suitable answers in a mild and pleasant tone, by which they seemed entirely disarmed of their rage and violence, although they had just before robbed and beat a man. And the one that had hitherto stood silent, being the most overcome, said to his fellow, 'Come, let's go. The Quakers go where they please.' And they, turning away, left us to pursue our journey without further interruption." (Journal, pp. 19-20)*

Later the same year, he fell so ill that "some of my Friends were ready to conclude I should not stay long with them." In the midst of his suffering, "a prospect opened on my mind to pay a religious visit to some parts of our island where no Friends lived." This led to alternating periods of commitment and doubt, paralleled by episodes of physical recovery and relapse. Finally one night, he had a vision that resolved his doubts (*Journal*, pp. 26-28). The following summer, with the permission of his monthly meeting, he carried out the promised journey and experienced elements of his vision fulfilled. (A fuller treatment of this vision and the subsequent trip is presented in the chapter, *Mystic*, below.)

This may have been the point at which his fate was sealed: Elias Hicks, Long Island farmer, was called by God to be a traveling minister. Over the next forty-eight years, he was to make more than fifty major trips and dozens of shorter ones in faithful response to divine leadings. He visited hundreds of Friends congregations from Virginia to Canada and west as far as Indiana. For those outside the religious society, he held scores of "public meetings."

Recognizing the obstacles people of color faced in attending mixed-race gatherings, he frequently held meetings for worship just among Native

Americans or for African-Americans - both enslaved and free. His face may well have been seen by more Americans - both inside and outside of the Society of Friends - than any other Quaker of his time.

There were gaps in his travels surrounding the deaths of his sons - six years around the passing of two older boys, two years at the time of his third son's death, and three more years when his youngest son died - otherwise, he traveled regularly in the ministry. This should not be taken as a sign of eagerness to be away from home. He often delayed leaving for months after receiving the blessing of his Friends at home and, while traveling, he frequently expressed the desire to return home. In a letter to Jemima on March 7, 1816, he wrote, "How we shall proceed from this place, I am not at present able to inform thee, as I have for a day or two past felt somewhat as though I should be released from much further service" (*Letters*, p. 28). He had been away from home since January 3rd - traveling north to Maine through winter weather. Contrary to his hopes, in the next three weeks he attended more than twenty additional Quaker meetings and public meetings, only reaching home on March 30th.

Part of his desire to return home was concern for Jemima. Although she seems to have been a capable farm manager, Elias worried his wife would overextend herself. As the years passed, his concern for her increased. In a letter home in 1817, he wrote:

> *"I may now add, my dear, the strong desire I feel for thy preservation, and that thou may not suffer thy temporal concerns to intrude upon either body or mind, so as to hinder or indispose [thee] from thy spiritual and better engagement. I would rather our outward concerns should suffer than that thou should fatigue either body or mind about them. Therefore, I would have thee consider that thy bodily strength is declining as thou advances in years, and will, of course, render bodily labor more and more oppressive. And surely, it cannot be consistent with divine wisdom that his noble creature, man, should be oppressed either to please himself or others." (Letters, p. 45)*

Being a farmer, it was easier to be away in the winter, but this brought on its own hardships. Caught in a March 1818 blizzard, he wrote, "We are at present prisoners and have been for several days past" (*Letters*, p. 69). Having gone four miles into the local village for an appointed meeting on a Saturday evening, he was forced by the weather to stay overnight. The next morning, the snow was so deep that he and his companions were unable to cover even three-quarters of a mile and had to retreat to the nearest house for lodging.

Even in these conditions, he kept his sense of humor. In his next letter to Jemima, he described how his carriage had overturned, throwing him and Valentine Hicks, his son-in-law and traveling companion, "in rather a sloughy place," adding that Valentine had also taken a spill the day before, "but no great harm came of it as he is still fat and healthy" (*Letters*, p. 73). Even so, his letters painted a clear picture of how physically and mentally demanding his travels were:

> *"My labor and exercise in the work I am engaged in, together with our quick passing from place to place, is as much as my bodily ability and strength of mind seems able to endure, as not only my arduous exercise in meetings from day to day and jolting on the roads – which for some time past have been very rough and uneven, being trod up very deep in this clay country in the open weather we have had some time past, but are now hard frozen, which makes the traveling nearly as tiresome as chopping or mowing. Add to that almost as soon as we retire from meetings to Friends' houses, many Friends gather to see us – wanting to be informed about many things. Insomuch that the intermediate time between meetings is almost as exercising to body and mind – in many instances – as is my arduous service in meetings, that I have no time to be idle. And even while I am writing these lines, pain and wearisomeness is my constant companion, having yesterday and this morning ridden near forty miles and had an arduous day's labor in meeting today, that had not the Lord been graciously near for my support, I should have failed ere now. But he has, through adorable mercy, been my strength and my song and carried me through and over every trial and supported me in all my arduous labor and travail to the praise of his grace, who is over all, blessed forever. Therefore, my dear, the query arises, 'What shall we render to the Lord for all his benefits? For his mercy is new every morning.'" (Letters, p. 64)*

Public Conflicts

Public meetings were appointed in a variety of venues – from taverns to legislative chambers – and frequently in another denomination's church building. Good manners might dictate a respectful approach to one's hosts, but not to Elias Hicks. Echoing the earliest Friends, he preached that Quakerism was the only true Christianity and Quaker practice was its only proper expression. The foreseeable results, of course, were public debates with local pastors and members of the congregation.

In one letter home, he was unable to disguise the delight he felt that "my being there before had made a great rumpus among the priests and some of their bigoted followers - which I was glad to hear was the case, being fully in the belief that it cannot be otherwise if Friends in the ministry preach our doctrines faithfully and honestly, without regarding the fear or favor of men." (*Letters*, p. 67)

Nor was he gentler in his times among Friends. He often commented that ministry to his fellow Quakers was both "to the comforting and instructing many minds, and administering reproof to the lukewarm, the licentious, and immoral" (*Journal*, p. 217). Such preaching was undoubtedly not welcomed by all.

Merely criticizing ordinary meeting members might have been acceptable to the local elders, but Hicks was willing to reproach even those in leadership positions. While visiting in Maine in the 1793, he noted:

> *"We passed on... to Berwick, where the Monthly Meeting for Dover was held the next day. It proved a very exercising season, great weakness attending the meeting by reason of the same rending, dividing spirit getting in among Friends... which appeared to make great havoc among them, insomuch that a great number of members had been separated and still were separating by denials from the monthly meeting. I had some close labor with them, not only by endeavors to stir up and warn the careless and refractory members, but also found it necessary to caution and warn those that had the chief management of discipline - believing they had too much departed from the meek Spirit of Jesus in ordering the affairs of Truth."(Journal, p. 53)*

This closely foreshadowed the discord awaiting the society thirty-five years in the future.

On occasion, his words may have been intemperate. In May 1822, Joseph Whitall, an experienced and respected Friend who had been the superintendent of Westtown School from 1811 to 1818, heard Hicks preach in a meeting for worship at the annual sessions of New York Yearly Meeting. According to Whitall, Hicks denied the divinity of Jesus Christ. Then, in late November of the same year, Hicks attended the Southern Quarterly Meeting in Philadelphia Yearly Meeting, where two members, Ezra Comfort and Isaiah Bell, said they, too, heard Hicks deny the divinity of Christ and make the claim that anyone could achieve the same divine status as Christ.[4]

Since Hicks spoke extemporaneously in worship, as led by the Spirit of God, it is impossible to know exactly what he said (note: his beliefs about Jesus will be discussed in a later chapter). When he was called to account by the Elders of Philadelphia Yearly Meeting, he denied the accusation. Nevertheless, they considered the charge to have merit and the resulting impasse became one more step on the road to separation.

Incidents like these contributed to ongoing conflict with the leadership of Philadelphia Yearly Meeting. Despite their ascendancy within that yearly meeting, the Elders could not control Elias Hicks. Increasingly, they viewed him as theologically unsound and an unwelcome interloper in their yearly meeting, but as a member of New York Yearly Meeting, Hicks was not subject to their jurisdiction. Complaints, such as those Whitall made, could only be judged by his home monthly and yearly meetings - and there he had broad support. This produced an escalating series of unresolved confrontations. One effect of these disputes was that the Philadelphians increasingly and publicly painted Hicks as spreading false doctrines and as the root cause of dissention.

Elias Hicks was, of course, not the only minister traveling among Friends in the early nineteenth century. Some itinerant ministers would later be found on each side of the Orthodox/Hicksite split, but most troublesome in Hicks' view was a continuous stream of evangelical Friends visiting in the United States from England in the years leading up to the separations. Hicks considered them "strangers and busybodies" who "spread death and darkness amongst us, and so interrupt our quiet by hard speeches that we have, as much as we can well do, patiently to endure" (*Letters*, p. 218).

This appeared in a letter to a close friend, William Poole, Jr., but it is unlikely such harsh words were restricted to his private correspondence. Such personal animosity may have contributed as much to the separations as the theological and doctrinal differences.

There had been, of course, substantial disagreements on matters of theology and doctrine within Quakerism from its first days, but these seemed unbridgeable. To Hicks' opponents, Unitarian and rationalist

---

[4] For a more complete description of these events, see H. Larry Ingle, *Quakers in Conflict: The Hicksite Reformation*. Wallingford, PA: Pendle Hill, 1998, pp. 105-115.

ideas were a foreign body being grafted into Quakerism. Similarly, Hicks viewed the introduction of evangelical theology as an intrusion of human innovations that stained the pure, primitive Christianity early Friends had revived. This put him at odds with those who called themselves "orthodox Friends." Moreover, he strenuously opposed what he saw as attempts to require that Quakers accept doctrines such as Trinitarianism and the primacy of the Bible as a rule and guide to life that early Friends had rejected. As Hicks viewed it, "a few envious individuals, letting in the spirit of jealousy, began to accuse their Friends of holding unsound doctrines without any just cause for so doing" (*Journal*, p. 415). Moreover, in his eyes, this constituted the imposition of a creed on the religious society. To the consternation of his opponents, he repeated these views in his public ministry. While he felt his message was a call for tolerance, the Orthodox saw it as an attack on essential Quaker principles.

The Last Journey

In his journal and letters, Elias Hicks reported little on the actual events in the divisions of 1827-28. He was not present for the proceedings at Philadelphia Yearly Meeting which tripped off the cascade of separations, but in 1828-29, he undertook the longest of his travels in the ministry. Leaving in late April 1828, the first portion of this journey took him as far as Richmond, Indiana. Along the way, he visited dozens of Quaker meetings and was present at Ohio Yearly Meeting when it split.

Although by that time, the National Road provided a paved surface that far west, he took a more demanding route across the mountains of Pennsylvania so he could visit with Quakers in the southwest of that state and northwest Ohio. On his way back to Long Island, he traveled through what is now West Virginia and Virginia before turning north to Baltimore, Philadelphia, and New York City. After more than seven months and about twenty-four hundred miles, he reached Jericho on January 24, 1829.

The Death of Jemima

A little over seven weeks later, on March 17, 1829, Jemima died of pneumonia – a greater burden than he had ever experienced before:

> *"We enjoyed sweet communion, both as to body and mind, for fifty-eight years and upwards, in which the declaration of our gracious Creator was verified in us, where he says, 'It is not good for man to dwell alone, I will make him a helpmeet' – such she was to me indeed. 'And the man shall*

leave father and mother and cleave unto his wife, and they shall no longer be twain, but shall be one flesh.' This precious and unbroken union was verified in our experience, which makes the trial greater. Yet I have cause for thankfulness and gratitude to the Blessed Author of all our sure mercies that he brought us together in his counsel, and united our hearts together by his love, and sustained us in the precious enjoyment thereof to old age – a period much longer than is generally experienced by the children of men. Which unmerited favor, I trust and hope, will preserve me from indulging one murmuring thought, but contrariwise, to thank God and take courage, still to press forward in the way everlasting, in full assurance that his mercy endureth forever." (Journal, p. 438)

At this point, he could easily have retired from his ministry, but he did not feel released from the work to which God had called him:

"On the 24th of 6th month 1829, I again left home with Cornell Willis for my companion to complete the visit to Friends and others in the compass of our yearly meeting – agreeable to a certificate I received from our monthly and quarterly meetings, expressive of their unity with me therein. This certificate I received in the spring of the year 1828." (Journal, p. 438)

The final leg of this last pilgrimage ended with an appointed meeting in Brooklyn, New York on November 16, 1829. Sitting in the audience at this, his last public meeting, was ten-year-old Walt Whitman. Hicks arrived at home two days later.

His Final Days

Elias Hicks survived the loss of his wife by less than a year. He had just finished writing a letter to an old friend, Hugh Judge, on February 14, 1830 when he suffered a debilitating stroke. He lingered for thirteen days, unable to leave his bed and incapable of speech, finally dying on February 27, 1830. The final words he wrote before he collapsed seem prescient:

"I will now draw to a close with just adding for thy encouragement, be of good cheer. For no new thing has happened to us, for it has ever been the lot of the righteous to pass through many trials and tribulations in their passage to that glorious and everlasting, peaceful and happy abode, where all sorrow and sighing end – the value of which is above all price. For when we have given all we can give and suffered all we can suffer, yet it is below its true value, for thou knows that that which costs us nothing is scarcely worth having.

"I will now conclude. And in the fullness of brotherly love and Christian fellowship, in which my family unites, to thee and thine, I subscribe, thy affectionate friend, as ever,

Elias Hicks

"Please to present my love to all Friends."

Things I Believe But Can't Prove

Hicks' Education

There is only one, very brief reference in his journal to Elias Hicks' own education. In the description of a dream he had when he was about seven years old, he stated he was "passing from school in my usual manner" (*Journal*, p. 3). As a farm boy in the middle of the eighteenth century, he might have attended classes for a few years at the local meeting school, when he was not needed at home. The death of his mother when he was about eleven years old might have marked the end of any formal education, but the fact he did precise and accurate surveying work indicates he could handle more than simple arithmetic.

Even more apparent, Elias Hicks was very well-read. It is not at all surprising he used arguments that had appeared in the works of George Fox, William Penn, or Robert Barclay - their books were well-known among Friends. Likewise, some of the imagery in his journal may have been inspired by the *Journal of John Woolman* (see the chapter, *Mystic*, below). What I had not anticipated was that he also quoted from non-Quaker sources. In one of his letters, he quotes from Percy Bysshe Shelley's *Prometheus Unbound* and Alexander Pope's *Epistles to Several Persons* (*Letters*, p. 99). Even more remarkable, Shelley's poem had first appeared in print only about a year before Hicks quoted from it.

It seems out of character for Hicks to have read the poem - not the least because Shelley was a notorious libertine - and I doubt Hicks ever perused a book of poetry. More likely, this is evidence Hicks at least occasionally read newspapers. In those days, empty space at the bottom of a column would be filled with a variety of material, including snippets of poetry.

The breadth of his reading was probably not unique among Quakers of that time. Friends might have wished to maintain a hedge, separating and protecting the religious society from the corrupting influences of the wider world, but the peoples of the world were all around them and did business with them every day. Even a farm that raised most of a family's own food sold excess crops and bought supplies and equipment - often from non-Quaker merchants. The industrial revolution was making things like mass-produced cloth so cheap that it didn't make sense to spin or weave.

The hedge, if it ever had worked, was being riddled with holes and Friends, including Elias Hicks, were peeking through.

The Eighteenth-Century Reformation

As discussed in the *Introduction*, an extensive reformation took place within the Religious Society of Friends in the middle of the eighteenth century that resulted in a smaller, but "purer" religious body. I believe this movement had important and lasting effects on Elias Hicks' concept of what it meant to be a Quaker. Since the reformation took place during Hicks' formative years, young Elias experienced the resulting more rigorous, Quietist society as "normal."

A lifetime of travel and reading a variety of material made him tolerant of those with different beliefs, but he still considered the society he knew in his youth to be normative Quakerism. A good Christian (which, in his mind, was the same as a good Quaker), surrendered utterly to the will of God - and sought knowledge of God's will by an absolute dependence on the guidance of the Inward Light of Christ. The result was a man who combined rigidity in the outward forms of Quakerism with a surprising degree of acceptance for doctrinal diversity.

Elias' & Jemima's Sons

It may also be noteworthy that it was in his teenage years Hicks was most lax in living up to Quaker standards. Although he reported living with his brother for only one summer, he devoted more pages in his journal to that summer "without restraint" and to related forms of misbehavior than to the whole rest of his youth. There is a telling comment interjected in his journal (p. 5) on "the great hurt many children receive by being too soon removed from under the watchful notice of their concerned parents." His own sons were struck down by a wasting disease at about the age Elias had been when his mother died and his wild years began.

As mentioned above, most likely his sons died from a genetic disorder passed on the X-chromosome - a disease I believe also killed their grandson, Elias Willets, and Jemima's brothers. Their boys - David, Elias Junior, Jonathan, and John - would have received this chromosome from their mother, who inherited it from her mother and passed it on to Elias Willets through her daughter, Phebe. Since women have two X-chromosomes, a recessive gene on that chromosome would not be expressed in a woman. But a man has only one X-chromosome and is vulnerable. Elias and Jemima, of course, lacked knowledge of genetics.

As a father, I know how I would feel if my daughters were healthy and my sons disabled. I would blame myself. For a man as steeped in scripture as Elias Hicks, it might have felt like "just retribution." The words of Exodus 34:7, where it says God "punishes the children and their children for the sin of the fathers" may have haunted him. Were his sons punished for the sins of his misspent adolescence?

That period of youthful wildness had ended when God, in a vision, confronted Elias on a dance floor. In essence, Hicks heard God say, "This is your last chance." I believe for the rest of his life Elias Hicks felt he was still on his last chance. So, when God said go, he had to go - even when he was old, tired, and worn.

There is another way in which the timing of his sons' deaths was particularly cruel. The oldest two, David and Elias Jr., would have begun to show signs of decline about the time the third son, Jonathan, was born and Elias Jr. died about a month after John, the youngest, was born. It is easy to envision Jemima and Elias hoping the younger two boys were replacements from a merciful God - just like Job, whose lost family was replaced with a new one in the final chapter. But it was not to be.

This painful timing was replayed with Elias Willets, who was born at about the time when his two remaining uncles began their own slow slides to death. Thankfully, the death of this grandson marked the end of their long trial.

Grieving

Elias Hicks had an obvious concern for the welfare of younger Friends and commented a number of times in his journal on the duties of parents. In these comments, he seems especially to worry about the guidance given to boys. To me, this reflects the sorrow he carried for the four sons he and

Jemima lost - sorrow he was otherwise unable to acknowledge. An early entry in his journal offers a notable example of this suppressed grief:

> *"When I have observed the great trouble and affliction that many parents have with undutiful children - especially their sons - when favored with health and strength to run at large, I could find very few parents but whose troubles and exercises in regard to their children far exceeded ours. And as their weakness and infirmity of body tended to preserve them in innocency and much out of the way of the troubles and temptations of the world, so we believe that in their deaths, they were happy and admitted into the realms of peace and joy - a reflection the most comfortable and joyous to parents of any in regard to their tender offspring."* (Journal, pp. 16-17)

The loss of each son brought on its own share of agony, but after describing in his journal (p. 16) how his sons died, Hicks added, "And I trust we were preserved from murmuring or repining thereat, as believing it to be dispensed in wisdom agreeable to the will and gracious disposing of an All-wise Providence for purposes best known to himself."

This may help explain why an eighty-year-old man - one who could reasonably have said he had already given all he could give and suffered all he could suffer - accepted the charge to once again travel thousands of miles over rough roads and no roads; through the heat and rains of summer, and the snow and cold of winter; even leaving home to finish the journey soon after his precious wife was taken from him.

Faithfulness wasn't just a vague theological concept or merely what others might say was required of him. Complete and utter submission to God's will was what Elias Hicks required of himself.

Jemima

Unfortunately, Jemima Seaman Hicks is an all-but-invisible figure in the documents available today. None of her letters have survived. In my opinion, she was the essential person in the life of Elias Hicks. Their marriage cemented him to the Society of Friends and made his travels among Friends possible. The life of a traveling minister required extra money and extra time. Marriage to Jemima provided both.

As mentioned above, Elias apprenticed as a carpenter - a useful profession and one that would likely have provided an adequate income to support a family - but the young United States was still a largely agrarian society. There was wealth for a few in the cities, but stability was best found in the soil. By marrying Jemima and within a few years, becoming the master of her parents' farm, he gained the ability not only to provide for her and their children, but to hope for a little surplus. Moreover, although farm work is demanding, it is seasonal. When he worked, he worked hard; but in the winter, the demands were lighter and he could more easily be away.

Even if the workload was lighter, someone needed to keep up with the off-season chores. Assistance came from a variety of sources. The Seaman-Hicks farm employed hired help, and at least some of these farm hands may have been longtime employees - there are instructions to "Josiah" in letters from 1797 and twenty-five years later in 1822. When Elias was older, he could also count on two sons-in-law, who lived in close proximity, to help out. In addition, each time Jericho Monthly Meeting issued a certificate allowing him to travel, they also accepted responsibility to look after his family and business while he was gone.

Another likely source of help was Elisabeth Hicks, their ninth child and fifth daughter. Never married, she seems to have lived with her parents until their deaths. She was educated at Nine Partners School and sent letters to her father when he was traveling, but none are in the archives of the Friends Historical Library of Swarthmore College and I have not found any elsewhere. She is referred to half a dozen times in the journal, traveling with her mother. Beyond these bare facts, I can find nothing, but I suspect she was a key support, and very likely took on much of the housework - and perhaps farm work - as her mother aged.

Above all, I believe Elias depended on Jemima to keep things in order at home. Remember her brothers all died before she was married. It is reasonable to suppose that from an early age she had pitched in everywhere on the farm - learning by practical experience from her mother how to be a farm wife, and from her father, to be a farmer.

Elias' faith in his wife is evident in a letter he sent her in 1818, "As to our affairs at home, I don't know that I can advise at present better than to leave them to be ordered in thy own discretion." (*Letters*, p. 63)

I can't prove it, but I believe without the love and practical support of Jemima Seaman Hicks, we may never have heard the name Elias Hicks.

Environmentalist

"We frequently err by the liberty we take in destroying what we esteem noxious creatures and not only abuse the power and rule given us over them by our great common Creator, but likewise act very contrary to and subversive of our own true interest." (Journal, p. 13)

It is anachronistic to refer to Elias Hicks as an environmentalist - the word "environment" was not used to refer to an ecological community until decades after his death. Nevertheless, he had a sense of the natural world and of humanity's place within it that is compatible with that of our modern environmental movement.

His language in referring to himself and to the natural world is instructive. He described himself as a creature living in creation - that is, one small part of a universe whose existence depended on a Creator. This flavors his view of humanity's role with respect to the earth. For Hicks, humans are stewards of the earth - that is, they are responsible for the care and maintenance of something that doesn't belong to them - "All our rich blessings are but the goods of our kind and gracious Benefactor and are only loaned to us during his good pleasure" (*Letters*, p. 182). And in the end, when we face our Creator, "we must give an account of our stewardship." (*Letters*, p. 33)

Shooting for Sport

As an old man compiling his journal, Hicks included a long meditation on creation and the proper place of humans in it. He remembered hunting alone as a boy and, "while waiting in stillness for the coming of the fowl, my mind hath been at times so taken up in divine meditations that they have been to me seasons of great instruction and comfort." He contrasted this with other times when, "in company with others on a party of pleasure... we have merely for sport and to try which could excel in shooting, fell upon the small, though innocent, birds... and destroyed many of them from wantonness or for mere diversion." More than sixty years later, he reflected, "For which cruel procedure my heart is sorrowfully affected whilst penning these lines." Such experiences led him to resolve "not to take the life of any creature, but such as were esteemed really useful when dead or very obnoxious and hurtful when living."

This apparently inspired the elderly memoirist to ponder more generally what humanity's place is within creation in a passage that shows uncommon appreciation for the roles of insects and predators:

> *"I have likewise… been led to believe that we frequently err by the liberty we take in destroying what we esteem noxious creatures and… act very contrary to and subversive of our own true interest. For no doubt, as all in the beginning was pronounced good that the good God had made, there was a right proportion and a true medium and balance among the creatures that were to inhabit this lower world. And man being made as a crown to the whole, no doubt his true interest lay in preserving, as much as might be, this true medium or balance.*
>
> *"But man… has wantonly fallen upon and destroyed such kinds as (to his limited understanding) appeared noxious because, at some times, they were observed to feed upon some of the fruits of the field that were the product of his industry – when a little care in frightening them away would have been sufficiently effectual and their lives preserved to fill up the place assigned them in creation. Hereby, the true balance has been so materially affected that the tribes of lesser creatures, such as reptiles and insects… have increased to a proportion sufficient to spread destruction and devastation over the fields and left the face of the earth, at times, as a scorched or barren desert.*
>
> *"… How presumptuous must it then appear from rational reflection for limited, borrowed beings to sport themselves with the lives of other beings? However little they may appear in the view of proud man (who vainly supposes all made for his use), yet they may be as necessary a link in the great chain of nature and creation as his own existence.*
>
> *"For although in the course of divine providence, we may be permitted to take the lives of such of the creatures (in a reasonable way) as are suitably adapted to the accommodation of our bodies in a line of real usefulness, yet that by no means carries any warrant for us wantonly, or in a sportive way, to destroy the lives of those that are not useful when dead… And had man kept his station as well as the other creatures, I have no doubt but the true balance would have been at least much better preserved than it now is – if not inviolably kept." (Journal, pp. 13-14)*

Contrast Hicks' use of "limited, borrowed beings" with "proud man" in the third paragraph above. The first phrase brings to mind how absolute human dependence is on God; while the second implies a haughty rejection of humanity's proper place.

A Farmer

Elias Hicks understood how humanity relates to the rest of creation in ways that few contemporary Quakers are able to do – as a farmer. And like many farmers, he could not conceive of a better way to live:

"What a vast portion of the joys and comforts of life do the idle and slothful deprive themselves of by running into cities and towns to avoid laboring in the field – not considering that that is the only true source that the gracious Creator of the universe has appointed to his creature, man – from whence to derive his greatest temporal happiness and delight, and which also opens the largest and best field of exercise to the contemplative mind, by which it may be prepared to meet (when this mortal puts on immortality) those immortal joys that will ever be the lot of the faithful and industrious." (Journal, pp. 191-92)

The agricultural year starts with planting and ends with the harvest. Success then (as today) depended on careful attention to crops and animals, but also on the mysterious workings of Providence. If it rains too much in the spring, the fields flood and seeds don't get in the ground. If the rains fail in the summer, there will be no harvest. All a farmer can do is to prepare as best she or he can and pray for divine assistance:

"I was closely engaged in preparing my fallow ground and sowing my wheat and rye – being willing to do my part carefully and industriously. And then I can with more confidence place my trust and dependence on a gracious and beneficent Providence for a blessing on my labor. For where care and industry are wanting, there is none for him to bless." (Journal, p. 195)

Keeping Animals

Farm animals are not pets or companions. In the nineteenth century, they were the motive power that plowed the fields and they provided food. Proper animal husbandry was more than a matter of kindness or of just meeting the family's needs, it was active stewardship:

"The rest of this week, I spent at home, being closely engaged in business and in making preparation for the more comfortable accommodation of my

stock through the inclemency of the approaching winter – considering that a merciful man is merciful to his beast – as I consider it not right to keep in my possession, and under my immediate notice, any more of the animal creation than I can render reasonably comfortable." (Journal, p. 163)

Unlike most living in the twenty-first century, if Hicks wanted to provide his family with meat, it required that he kill and butcher one of his animals. This had been part of his life since he was born, but it didn't harden him to the realities involved. On the last day of 1813, he and some of his farm hands spent the day laying up beef for the winter. In the evening, he reflected on the day's work in his home journal:

"Spent part of this day and the evening in assisting my workmen in slaying a fat beef and laying it away for part of our winter's provision. After which, my mind was seriously impressed with the subject and led to take a view of the whole process and the extraordinary change that had taken place in so short a space with a strong, well-favored, living animal, that in the morning was in a state of health, vigor, and comely proportion, and at the close of the evening, all its parts were decomposed, and its flesh and bones cut into pieces and packed away in a cask with salt to be devoured by the animal-man – its entrails already devoured by the swine, and its skin deposited with the tanner to be converted into leather for man's use.

"What a wonderful wreck in nature, affected in so short a period by two or three individuals, but which cannot be restored to its former state by all the combined power and wisdom of all the men in the universe, through all the ages and generations of men.

"My meditation hereon produced this query: Is it right, and consistent with divine wisdom, that such cruel force should be employed and such a mighty sacrifice be made necessary for the nourishment and support of these bodies of clay? Or is there not a more innocent and more consistent medium to be found, amply to effect the same end of man's support? And if so, will it not become a duty? If not for the present generation, for those in future to seek it and employ it." (Journal, pp. 169-70)

Harvest

The harvest is the hardest and most precarious time of year for a farmer. When the weather is uncooperative, it may only cost a single day of work missed, but if it turns really bad, a year's bounty can be lost entirely. With fair weather, work starts before the sun is up and doesn't end when it sets again. In the days before air conditioned tractors and combines the size of small houses, bringing in the crop required human muscle power, too. Even as he aged, Hicks seems to have genuinely enjoyed the demanding, physical labor; and work in the fields renewed thoughts of his connections to the natural world:

> *"Labored hard in my harvest field. And although sixty-six years of age, I found I could wield the scythe and cradle nearly as in the days of my youth. And it was a day of thankful and delightful contemplation – my heart was filled with thankfulness and gratitude to the Blessed Author of my existence in a consideration of his providential care over me in preserving me in health and in the possession of my bodily powers... but also in contemplating the works of nature and providence, in the blessings and beauties of the field – a volume containing more delightful and profitable instruction than all the volumes of latter learning and science in the world." (Journal, p. 191)*

Things I Believe But Can't Prove

Having spent parts of my own adolescent summers on my grandfather's farm in western New York, I feel a special connection to this aspect of Elias Hicks. I stood on the back of a potato digger as big as a machine shed and picked out the rocks as a seemingly endless stream of fresh-dug earth, plant tops, and potatoes passed in front of me. Mindless, hard, physical farm labor lent itself to contemplation – even for a twentieth-century teenager.

If Elias Hicks were to return today, I think he would seek out the few remaining Quaker meetings in agricultural areas. Even with all the new devices, the essence of farm life hasn't changed. He would be right at home.

Challenges

As will be seen in the chapter, *Applied Quakerism*, Hicks was very skeptical of collective actions, especially when they involved joint activities with those who are not Friends. As such, while he would probably share and admire the goals of today's environmental movement, he would probably question the ways in which they are being pursued.

Certainly, just writing a check would not be sufficient. Whenever there is a concern to be addressed, Friends need to face it directly in our own lives. Before joining a committee or supporting a broader organization, each needs to consider what God is leading him or her to do as an individual. This might result in communal action, but it would start with a very personal examination of everyday activities.

The words and example of John Woolman are enlightening in this respect. In *A Plea for the Poor*, Woolman wrote about the roots of war and what was required of those who oppose it. This was not a call to start a peace movement, but for self-examination and personal transformation:

> *"Oh, that we who declare against wars and acknowledge our trust to be in God only, may walk in the light, and therein examine our foundation and motives in holding great estates! May we look upon our treasures and the furniture of our houses and the garments in which we array ourselves and try whether the seeds of war have nourishment in these our possessions or not. Holding treasures in the self-pleasing spirit is a strong plant, the fruit whereof ripens fast. A day of outward distress is coming, and Divine love calls to prepare against it!"*[1]

In the same way, when Hicks felt a divine call to oppose slavery, he didn't join an abolition society - although many of his Friends did. He was a preacher, so he first used those gifts to witness forcefully - and directly to slaveholders - on the evils it embodied. He called on them to look upon their own treasures and to acknowledge they had been stolen from those they held in bondage. Then he challenged everyone else to consider the privileges they enjoyed because of the slave system. That done, he also called on Friends to act corporately by petitioning the government on behalf of all those cruelly held in bondage.

I think today, Hicks would challenge us to "look upon our treasures" - furniture, air conditioning, foods imported from around the world, cars (even hybrids), and the garments sewn in third-world factories - and "try whether the seeds" of global warming have nourishment in these or not.

Do we first put our own lives in order before calling on others to change?

Do we heedlessly accept the benefits of others' bad environmental behaviors?

---

[1] Moulton, Phillips P. (Ed.), *The Journal and Major Essays of John Woolman*, New York: Oxford University Press, 1971, p. 255.

Mystic

"How deep and solemn are thy obligations to the God of thy salvation! How hath he often taken thee out of the horrible pit and out of the miry clay, and set thee upon a rock and put a new song into thy mouth – even praises, high praises to him!" (Journal, p. 101)

At his death in 1772, John Woolman left several manuscripts of his journal. A committee of Friends from Philadelphia Yearly Meeting was tasked with assembling the various pieces into a book for publication. When the first edition of *A Journal of the Life, Gospel-Labours, and Christian Experiences, of that Faithful Minister of Jesus Christ, John Woolman* was published in 1774, all his dreams had been edited out. A complete edition of the journal, including all his dreams and visions, was not published for almost two hundred years.

Half a century later, following the death of Elias Hicks, a committee of Friends from the Hicksite New York Yearly Meeting took on the task of preparing his manuscript memoirs for publication. The resulting 1832 edition of Elias Hicks' journal was edited down considerably - about one-quarter of the manuscript material was excised. Tellingly, the few dreams and visions Hicks had included were deleted.

There is no way to know why those Friends decided to delete the dreams and visions in either journal. If the changes had been unique to Hicks, the reasons behind them might relate to him alone, but the fact that the journal of a Quaker as revered as Woolman was similarly rewritten - and it took so long for the material to be restored - points beyond the individuals. Likewise, the fact that two different committees, separated geographically and in time, both eliminated the same kind of material suggests a more general, negative attitude towards mystical experiences in the Religious Society of Friends of the late-eighteenth and early-nineteenth centuries. The simplest explanation may be that (in the presence of strangers) Quakers were not supposed to have dreams and visions. If so, by removing them from the published journals, the editors spared John

Woolman and Elias Hicks embarrassment; and by association, shielded the Religious Society of Friends from shame. The acrimony that flowed from the Hicksite/Orthodox separations might have made this all the more important to Hicks' literary executors.

By their nature, mystical experiences require interpretation and that can be highly subjective. Below, the whole of several will be presented, along with speculation on its meaning for Elias Hicks. More than any other chapter, this one calls on the reader to engage with what Hicks wrote and come to his or her own conclusions.

A Day of Visitation

One vision in particular was of fundamental importance to the course of the life of Elias Hicks, but was hidden in the 1832 edition of the journal and is still only partially available today. This vision probably occurred in his late teens and marks a break in the trajectory of his life. He had fallen into company with a group of other young men who enjoyed life in ways a young Quaker needed to avoid - apparently including sex with willing young women (*Journal*, p. 7). In a single moment, he was made aware of the state of his life and asked to choose his future. The manuscript pages describing this event are missing from the Swarthmore archives. I suspect they were destroyed by the journal's editorial committee, but Hicks had shared the story with others in his home meeting. After his death, their memorial minute for him contained the following:

> *"On one occasion, when preparing to join in the dance, and surrounded by his jovial companions, the pure witness rose so powerfully in his mind, and so clearly set before him the evil tendency of the course he was pursuing, that he reasoned not with flesh and blood, but gave up to the heavenly vision, and in deep contrition and prostration of soul, entered into covenant with the God of his life, that if he would be pleased to furnish him with strength, he would endeavor not to be again found in the like disobedience; which covenant, through mercy, he was favored to keep inviolate." (Journal, p. 9)*

The 1832 edition of the journal has no mention of a vision. Instead, Hicks was portrayed as realizing his situation and deciding, with God's help, to change his life. It is recognizably the same incident, but with a rational, rather than a mystical description of the experience.

A Great Ball of Fire

The first experience reported in the journal was "a night vision, when about seven years of age." This certainly wasn't his earliest dream nor is it described as the first to which he attached special import, but it must have had deep significance for him - three-quarters of a century later, he included it in his memoirs:

> *"I apprehended I was passing from school in my usual manner. Passing by a certain hedge on the way, there was a lopped tree with a hollow in it, wherein, a little bird called the wren sometimes had eggs. Turning into the hedge in quest thereof, as I looked into the hole in the tree and was about to put in my hand to feel for eggs, I thought I beheld the face of an angel as I had seen them described by pictures in a book – the first prospect whereof struck me with terror as one guilty – and immediately thereupon, I thought there issued a flame out of the hollow of the tree and it enclosed me about, as a round ball or blaze of pure fire of about eight feet diameter, which struck me with great amazement and horror. Turning around to look for some relief, I apprehended I saw my father, standing just without the flame, to whom I thought I cried with vehemence, but he appeared to be entirely calm and looked upon me without any show of concern. He very gently requested me to be still, which tended gradually to center my mind and compose it. In this situation I awoke, feeling a very agreeable and comfortable warmth, which together with finding myself safe in my bed, was cause of great gladness.*
>
> *"Nevertheless, the vision continued with me at times for years and was an excellent memento [reminder] and I believe had a tendency to preserve me from many temptations in my childhood and youth, for when after I was tempted to evil, this vision would often come up fresh in view and strengthen [me] to resist, for fear of the fatal consequence." (Journal, p. 3)*

To me, this dream is about the omniscience and mercy of God. No matter where or when, God (as symbolized by the angel) knows and sees each of us and knows what we are doing. The ball of fire threatens punishment - the eternal fires of hell - but that punishment was stayed by the comforting presence of his earthly father - standing in for his all-merciful heavenly Father. For Hicks, this was humanity's condition in this life - to live under the constant, merciful, and loving gaze of God. The dream likewise modeled the appropriate response, "to be still, which tended gradually to center my mind and compose it."

The dream has several interesting parallels to a story told by John Woolman. Early in his journal, Woolman gave an account of walking to a neighbor's house as a boy. Along the way, he noticed a robin sitting on a nest in a tree.

When young John approached, the robin flew about - trying to distract him from the hatchlings in her nest. Being a boy, Woolman threw rocks at the bird, one of which struck and killed her. Although he was initially pleased with himself, he was soon horrified to think the young robins would slowly starve to death. He could not leave them to that fate. To prevent it, he climbed up to the nest and killed the chicks.[1]

The presence of this story so early in his journal is a measure of how formative an event it was. Woolman's journal was widely available among Friends and Elias Hicks probably read it. In fact, Woolman's story of a robin may have prompted Hicks to remember and write about his own dream of a wren.

A Vision of Paying a Religious Visit

Another transformative vision occurred when Hicks was thirty-three years old. He had already been recognized as a minister by Jericho Meeting and traveled to Philadelphia at the request of his yearly meeting, but he had not yet felt a divine leading to travel among Friends.

Hicks was seriously ill - some friends even worried he would die - and, like many sick people, he offered God a bargain. If he recovered, he promised to "pay a religious visit to some parts of our island where no Friends lived." But as he improved, he had second thoughts - as many people do - bringing on "distress and anxiety of spirit." Cycles of commitment and reconsideration continued, until a resolving vision came to him:

> *"In the fall of this year, 1781, I was taken with a fever which held me for several months, in the course of which, my natural strength became very much exhausted and... when I was reduced nearly to the lowest state of bodily weakness during my complaint, a prospect opened on my mind to pay a religious visit to some parts of our island where no Friends lived and among a people who, from the acquaintance I had with them, appeared*

---

[1] *A Journal of the Life, Gospel-Labours, and Christian Experiences, of that Faithful Minister of Jesus Christ, John Woolman* in *Works of John Woolman*, Philadelphia: Printed by Joseph Crukshank, 1774, p. 5.

more likely to make a ridicule of me than to receive me or my doctrine... After long struggling and pleading to be released without any the least prospect of obtaining my desire, I at length yielded to the heavenly call – which brought immediate peace and comfort to my afflicted soul...

"But after a little time of quiet, in which at times I had again to view the prospect and look at the difficulties that appeared many ways likely to attend the putting it in practice... These considerations brought renewed exercise and caused me several times during the time of my recovery to recant and draw back. And then, nothing but distress and anxiety of spirit was my portion until I again resigned thereto. And the Lord was very gracious – opening many things for my encouragement.

"And one night, as I was musing on the subject in some distress of mind and getting a little quiet, I fell asleep, but seemed in vision to be in a great ecstasy in regard to performing the visit and thought I was in the east side of the town where I was to have the first meeting. I thought, in the anguish of my spirit, I cried out aloud, 'Where should I go to find a house for a meeting?' And I apprehended I saw a black man standing a little from me who had heard my cry and calling to me says, 'Here, I will show thee the house.' And stretching out his hand, pointed across to the south at part of the town and seemed to direct my sight to a particular spot. Although I knew not at that time anything of the place or whether there was a house there or not, but it quite eased my mind and I awoke, and felt comfortable, and ever after felt resigned to the prospect." (Journal, pp. 26-28)

Although it brought resolution to his distress – both physical and spiritual – Hicks kept this vision to himself and he didn't approach his monthly meeting for permission to make the journey until about half a year later, "in the forepart of the next summer." The meeting gave its approval and named two elders to accompany him. Even then, he delayed leaving until "about the middle of the 8th month 1782." The 1832 edition of his journal contains his request to travel, but omits this description of the trip itself:

"The first place that opened for a meeting was the town of Jamaica and when we came into the east part of the town, where (as expressed before) I thought I saw a black man directing me where to go, my dream came fresh in my mind and the prospect seemed as plain to me now as it did in the vision – but I had not opened it to my Friends and they proposed to go to a different part of the town. And I assayed to go with them, but when I passed the street that led to the place pointed to by the black man, I felt a

stop in my mind and told Friends it felt most right to me to go down thither, to which they readily consented. And when I came in sight of the spot where my mind seemed directed in the vision, there stood a house thereon, but not knowing who lived in it, it was proposed to go on some distance further to a house of our acquaintance. But when I attempted to pass the aforesaid house, I felt again a full stop in my mind and told Friends I believed we must go to that house. Accordingly, we went and when we came in, the man (though a stranger) received us courteously, and when we informed him our business and that we had a desire to have a religious opportunity with the neighbors, he freely offered us his house, which at this juncture was rendered convenient for a meeting by a new addition which he had built to a shop adjoining – he being a trader – and in which the next day, he had expected to have deposited his goods, but would put it off one day longer to make way for the meeting.

"And while we were conversing on the subject of the meeting, in stepped a religious black man and when he found there was a prospect of a meeting, he seemed to leap for joy and spake out and says, 'I will go and give notice,' and spake very encouragingly to the subject – the consideration whereof, and things turning so very agreeable to my prospect, made deep impressions of thankfulness and gratitude on my mind. After which, I opened to my Friends the prospect I before had seen of this place and how everything had turned out agreeable thereto, which had likewise a very strengthening and encouraging effect on their minds.

"Accordingly the next day, we had a very favored meeting with a considerable number of the inhabitants who came in and behaved soberly." (Journal, pp. 28-29)

Having his vision fulfilled seems to have resolved any remaining doubts Hicks harbored about being called to a traveling ministry.

A Vision of a Rainbow

The next vision came to him on March 20, 1798 while he was traveling in Virginia. The journey had been long – over three months so far and he had yet to turn back towards home. He was tired, but as things turned out, he had a long way yet to travel. It would be late May before he was back in Jericho.

The previous day, he had attended a quarterly meeting in Fairfax and he was discouraged. One of the informal functions of quarterly meetings in the eighteenth century was as a marriage market – young people from meetings spread over a moderate geographic area (roughly all within a day's ride) got a chance to spend time together - but things were apparently out of hand. Hicks was circumspect, saying only "it had become more hurtful than beneficial by reason of the great concourse of idle people coming together at that time - not so much for the sake of the meeting, as to see and be seen, and making it a place of diversion" (*Journal*, p. 75). This was heavy on his heart that night:

> *"About the middle of the night, I awoke and my sleep went from me, and my mind was brought into a state of deep exercise and travail from a sense of the great turning away of many among us from the law and testimony, and the prevailing of a spirit of great infidelity and deism among the people, and darkness spreading over the minds of many as a thick veil... and, in the anguish of my spirit, I said, 'Lord, spare thy people and give not thy heritage to reproach and suffer not thy truth to fall in the streets.' And after having spread my supplication before him after this manner, and acknowledged with gratitude his multiplied mercies, my mind was made easy and I fell into a sweet sleep.*
>
> *"And in vision, there opened before me the appearance of a bright rainbow that extended from one side of the horizon to the other, through the zenith from the northwest to the southeast, and in a seeming soft language, it revived on my mind, this is the token of the covenant that God made with his people, that he would not again destroy the world with a flood. Great Babylon was now brought into remembrance before God and her cup was full and her fall was near at hand, and that the Lord is now arising and will give her, her due.*
>
> *"And I awoke and my mind was much comforted in the prospect, believing that the vision was true, and the interpretation thereof sure - that the Kingdom of Antichrist had now got near to its height. That Satan (or the man of sin) had laid his top-stone by leading his votaries to an open acknowledgement of their disbelief." (Journal, pp. 77-78)*

Hicks was a child of the mid-eighteenth-century Quaker reformation. In the early nineteenth century, he saw apostasy creeping into his beloved society. This dream was a reminder that God is constant and dependable, even if God's people are not.

Thirty years later, he included this happy and optimistic prospect in his memoirs.

Stepping Stones in a Miry Bog

The final vision reported in his journal came to Hicks while he was in a meeting for worship. Again, he was away from home. He had departed in October 1818 for seven weeks, rested at home for three weeks, and then resumed his travels for another fourteen weeks - finally returning home on April 8, 1819. From his description, it was an easier time spiritually than he had twenty years earlier in Virginia (above), but he was now seventy years old and the constant winter travel must have been wearying.

He attended morning worship at the Friends Meeting in Athens, New York on March 28, 1819. The experience described below came during a public meeting he had appointed for non-Quakers in the afternoon of the same day. In this mystical encounter, the immediate presence of the Holy Spirit led him in offering ministry:

"A great power of darkness seemed so to prevail, as entirely for a considerable time to close up and block the way to any public service. But as I patiently submitted to the baptism and willingly became baptized with and for the dead - as it is only through death that the resurrection from death can be witnessed - a little glimmering of light appeared, in which I felt the necessity of standing up, but with the utmost caution to mind the stepping stones. For my way (for a time) was like passing through a miry bog, enclosed with mist and darkness, with but just light enough to see the way - and that composed of stepping stones, and but one visible at a time. And when I had taken one step and found it to be solid and sure, I had then to look carefully for the next. And as I thus proceeded, keeping my eye single to the light that led the way, the light more and more arose out of obscurity and the darkness vanished. And he that opens and none can shut, and shuts and none but himself can open, made way for the promotion of his own righteous cause and the exaltation of Truth's testimonies." (Journal, p. 361)

This image of picking his way step-by-step through a miry bog closely paralleled a passage from John Woolman's journal in which Woolman was also describing the experience of being guided to offer vocal ministry. The following is taken from an edition of Woolman's journal that would have been available in Hicks' lifetime:

"I have sometimes felt a Necessity to stand up; but that Spirit which is of the World hath so much prevailed in many, and the pure Life of Truth been so pressed down, that I have gone forward, not as one travelling in a Road

cast up and well prepared, but as a Man walking through a Miry-place, in which are Stones here and there, safe to step on, but so situated, that, one Step being taken, Time is necessary to see where to step next."[2]

As mentioned above, Elias Hicks likely read John Woolman's journal. This imagery seems to have spoken to Hicks' condition as he sat that afternoon in silent worship and stayed with him for years after.

Hints of Other Visions

Hicks only recorded a few dreams and visions in his memoirs and mentions none in his letters, but there are hints others occurred and that he gave appreciable weight to them. The most direct indication of other experiences is recorded early in the journal (p. 17):

"Being about the twenty-sixth year of my age... I was led through adorable mercy to see that although I had ceased from many sins and vanities of my youth, yet there were many remaining that I was still guilty of, that had not as yet been atoned for, and for which I now felt the judgments of God to rest upon me. And a sense whereof caused me to cry mightily to the Lord for pardon and redemption, and he graciously condescended to hear my cry and to open my way before me wherein I must walk in order to experience reconciliation with him. As I abode in watchfulness and deep humiliation before him, light brake forth out of obscurity, and my darkness became as the noonday, and I had many deep openings in the visions of light – greatly strengthening and establishing to my exercised mind."

Challenges

Although Hicks never directly addressed the issue, I believe he presumed preternatural experiences could originate in either good or evil. He had no doubt about the reality of Satan, devils, and other demons – when in 1829 he was challenged about the existence of such entities, he responded, "the Scriptures tell us there are many of them, and that Jesus cast seven out of one woman" (*Letters*, p. 258). Satan is a deceiver – appearing as "an angel of light – by which he lies in wait to deceive, and has generally deceived, and still deceives, the greater part of the people of all the nations under heaven." (*Journal*, p. 296)

---

[2] *A Journal of the Life, Gospel-Labours, and Christian Experiences, of that Faithful Minister of Jesus Christ, John Woolman* in *Works of John Woolman*, Philadelphia: Printed by Joseph Crukshank, 1774, p. 221

Accordingly, he knew he could never naively assume any vision, dream, or leading necessarily afforded divine guidance. If he were with us today, Hicks would warn that these may originate in the Tempter - although twenty-first-century Friends might identify the source with the ego.

In either case, people are tempted to trust in their own judgment too much when careful discernment is required. This would include testing a sense of being led with one's own spiritual community to be sure of its provenance. To do this, Hicks would advise, requires humility, but the products of such work are of immeasurable value.

People often approach others to request support for what they have already decided to do, not to find clearness on whether "the vision was true, and the interpretation thereof sure."

Do we have the humility to test our dreams and visions, i.e., to submit our leadings to the discernment of our spiritual communities?

Scripture

"[Today, I] Spent mostly in my temporal business, but not without a watchful care lest it should engage too much of my attention. The evenings were partly spent in reading the scriptures, in which I greatly delight. How excellent are those records. Although old, yet seem ever new."
(Journal, p. 168)

To truly understand Elias Hicks, one has to appreciate the role of the Bible in his life. He reported in his journal (p. 8) he began to read at an early age and "took considerable delight in reading the Scriptures." Love of the Bible was not unusual for a Quaker. From the days of George Fox, Robert Barclay, and William Penn, Friends read scripture often and diligently. As in the writings of those Friends, Hicks' were richly infused with quotes, paraphrases, citations, and allusions to the Bible.

From their earliest days, Friends found the Bible to be more than just an entertaining book of ancient stories and a source of pithy quotes. Scripture was composed by the inspiration of the Holy Spirit. As such, it has great weight, although second to the Holy Spirit in authority. What's more, readers need to open themselves to that inspiration - allowing that same Inspiring Spirit to reveal hidden and underlying meanings - in order to rightly understand it. In an 1829 letter to Charles Stokes, Hicks gave a précis of his views:

> *"First, as to the Scriptures of Truth as recorded in the book called the Bible, I have ever believed that all parts of them that could not be known but by revelation were written by holy men as they were inspired by the Holy Ghost and could not be known through any other medium. And they are profitable for our encouragement, comfort, and instruction in the very way that the apostle Paul testifies. And I have always accounted them, when rightly understood, as the best of books extant. I have always delighted in reading them in my serious moments - in preference to any other book from my youth up - and have made more use of their contents to confirm and establish my ministerial labors in the gospel than most other ministers*

that I am acquainted with. But at the same time, I prize that from whence they have derived their origin much higher than I do them – 'As that for which a thing is such, the thing itself is more such.' And no man (I conceive) can know or rightly profit by them, but by the opening of the same inspiring Spirit by which they were written. And I apprehend that I have read them as much as most other men and none, I believe, has received more profit from them than I have." (Letters, p. 256)

Stokes was expected to recognize, "As that for which a thing is such, the thing itself is more such" as a quote from the third proposition, "Of the Scriptures," in Robert Barclay's Quaker classic, *An Apology for the True Christian Divinity.*[1] To put it in simple terms, no matter how great the value of the scriptures, the Spirit that inspired them is greater.

The Purpose of the Bible

Note first in this statement, Elias Hicks almost directly quoted the description of the role the Bible claims for itself in 2 Timothy 3:16 ("All scripture is given by inspiration of God, and is profitable for doctrine, for reproof, for correction, for instruction in righteousness."). He accepted this as unquestionably true.

Scripture is Divinely Inspired

Consistent with Christian tradition, Hicks believed the Bible was divinely inspired. Some parts of it are first person accounts of a writer's own experience, but that cannot always have been the case. For example, the book of Job reports conversations in heaven between God and Satan which could not have been witnessed by an earth-bound author. To Hicks, these sections weren't just invented by the author – "all parts of them that could not be known but by revelation were written by holy men as they were inspired by the Holy Ghost."

If, as many Protestants claim, the age of inspiration has ended, only this outward product would be available to direct human actions, but Friends believe readers also receive inspired guidance – "no man (I conceive) can know or rightly profit by them, but by the opening of the same inspiring Spirit by which they were written." In other words,

---

[1] Barclay, Robert, "An Apology For The True Christian Divinity, As The Same Is Held Forth And Preached By The People Called Quakers," in *Truth Triumphant: Through the Spiritual Warfare, Christian Labours, and Writings, of that Able and Faithful Servant of Jesus Christ, Robert Barclay.* London: Thomas Northcott, 1692.

understanding the meaning of a passage is not merely an intellectual exercise; it is first and foremost a spiritual one. In this way, old revelations can be newly revealed to the inspired reader.

The Bible is Not the Ultimate Rule and Guide

Nearly all Protestants in the nineteenth century held the Bible to be the ultimate rule and guide to life; and in the years leading up to the Great Separations of 1827-28, some evangelically-influenced Quakers began to espouse that theological position. Hicks stood firmly with the earliest Friends - the written text has less authority than the ultimate origin of that text, the Holy Spirit. While the Bible is undoubtedly the best outward resource available, the inward illumination of the Light of Christ is the ultimate rule and guide. This is discussed in more detail in the chapter, *Faithfulness and the Inward Light.*

The Dangers of Bibliolatry

From their earliest days, Friends have denounced the practice they saw as common among Protestants of raising the Bible above its proper place. They saw this as a form of idolatry - i.e., raising up a thing made with human hands and putting it in God's proper place. Elias Hicks was well aware of this standard and, when attacked for his views on scripture, he cited it as part of his defense:

> *"George Fox was raised up to bear testimony to the Light and Spirit of Truth in the hearts and consciences of men and women as the only sure rule of faith and practice - both in relation to religious and moral things - and which was complete and sufficient without the aid of books or men, as his doctrine and example clearly evinces, as his reformation was begun and carried on without the necessary aid of either. But as the professors of Christianity, then held the Scriptures (or their interpretations of them) as their chief idol - and such was their veneration for them that, for anyone to hold up anything else as a rule, he was immediately pronounced as a heretic or schismatic and not fit to company or associate with in any way." (Letters, p. 55)*

That bit of history did not protect Hicks from condemnation. He was, in the eyes of his accusers, denigrating the only infallible guide available to humanity. When some of these Friends advocated the practice of regular Bible reading at predetermined times, Hicks denounced it as "an innovation" - in those days, "innovation" was Quaker code for importing a custom foreign to Friends' beliefs. Hicks trusted to the immediate guidance of the Inward Light to direct people when to read scripture and when to read or to do something else.

"Another complaint thou mentionest is that I 'counteract our discipline respecting reading the Scriptures,' which is also a mistake, as my mind is the same – to encourage Friends, especially the younger class – as I have always done in that respect. But I have only endeavored to counteract the innovations that appear in many Friends, by fixing times beforehand...

"All that is good within me abominates such superstitious conduct. I consider our discipline goes no further and means no more than that Friends carefully endeavor, by every right means, to inculcate right ideas of morality and religion in the minds of their children and their families. And believing that by sometimes reading the Scriptures and other good books at intervals (when nothing better offers), they prove as an auxiliary, they recommend them accordingly – but have fixed no times for it... For it will remain an eternal truth, that the letter killeth, but the spirit only giveth life." (Letters, pp. 97-98)

Gospel Law is Inward – The Scriptures are Outward

The Bible is a visible product of an invisible source – a source to which each person has direct and equal access. For Hicks, anything outward was necessarily inferior to the spiritual reality found within the heart of each person – the only thing "reading the scriptures or hearing the gospel preached... can do for any man is only to point to and lead the minds of the children of men home to this divine inward principle, manifested in their own hearts and minds." (*Journal*, p. 314)

Inscribed in each person's heart is gospel law. This is not Law in the Old Testament sense – a "shalt" and "shalt not" list – but God's unique calling for each individual:

"The gospel law is inward and spiritual, and cannot be comprehended in outward characters, but must be written in every heart distinctly [Hebrews 8:10]. As our states and conditions are all different and distinct from each other, so the law of God is distinct in every heart, and is always suited to the state and condition of every heart, and of course must act diversely in each mind, according to the diversity of their several dispositions, propensities, and passions. Therefore no literal law or creed can take place under the gospel – except in moral or outward things – for

no outward law can bind the soul, as the government of the soul is exclusively the prerogative of God and not of man." (Letters, p. 183)

Hicks insisted scripture pointed each man and woman to the workings of an infallible guide within his or her own heart. For Hicks, this called for profound personal commitment to faithfully follow the specific leadings of the Inward Light. It meant accepting the burden of personal responsibility for one's spiritual life. But for other Friends - notably those who would become Orthodox - this was a prescription for spiritual anarchy.

Problems of Interpretation

One elementary problem was stated above in the letter to Charles Stokes, "I have always accounted them, when rightly understood, as the best of books extant." The critical words are "when rightly understood." If each person interpreted a passage as he or she felt led, who was to say how a passage was to be rightly understood? The traditional answer to this query was God is One and, therefore, all who faithfully read the scripture under divine guidance would be led to the same interpretation. Friends on both sides of the Great Separations held this view, but it didn't prevent schism.

Hicks understood interpretation is always conducted in a context. First of all, each part of the Bible was produced by a limited human being writing at a particular time and to address issues that were important to a particular people. In keeping with the beliefs of his day, Hicks trusted that Moses wrote the first five books, the Pentateuch, for the children of Israel; and David composed the Psalms. In the New Testament, he assumed Paul wrote all the epistles attributed to him. Hicks felt assured the message in each book was exactly what the people addressed needed at that time. But, he wondered, is it what is needed today? Of that, he was skeptical:

"I have no doubt but when the apostle, under the influence of Divine Love, addressed an epistle to the Corinthians, that he was rightly directed therein. And as he knew and was led into a right knowledge of their states, so he could administer to their needs and to their instruction. But I don't apprehend that he had the most distant idea that he was writing to nations yet unborn, and of whose states and conditions he could have no knowledge. Nor do I believe that Divine Wisdom had any design, when he influenced the mind of the apostle to write his several epistles to the Corinthians, that he intended them for after-ages." (Letters, p. 183)

Moreover, Hicks was aware that English was not the original language. Speaking of the necessary translators, he wrote, "We have no certainty that they have given us the apostle's sense clearly" (*Letters*, p. 81). He was similarly dubious that the many transcriptions made over the course of centuries had all been letter-for-letter accurate.

He even suggested some changes to the inspired texts had been intentionally introduced. In discussing the trinity, he noted the word "trinity" never occurs in scripture and "there is but one mention of it in Scripture and that, no doubt, is an interpolation" (*Letters*, pp. 202-03). This "mention" is 1 John 5:7 in the King James Version, "For there are three that bear record in heaven, the Father, the Word, and the Holy Ghost: and these three are one."

This was a view shared by some scripture scholars in the 1820s, who believed this verse had been deliberately altered sometime after the epistle was first composed. They apparently were right. Most modern translations reduce this verse and the next to "For there are three that testify: the Spirit, the water and the blood; and the three are in agreement."

Translation and transcription errors might be eliminated if the original manuscripts could be found, but even then, there would still be problems. Contradictions between and within the texts are obvious to every conscientious reader, including Elias Hicks:

> *"For would not some of us be very glad if we could have immediate access to Paul and some other of the apostles, who contradict one another and sometimes themselves – by which means we might be informed of the true meaning of what they wrote, and cause us all to understand them alike." (Letters, pp. 96-97)*

Lacking access to the apostles, who was to say how a passage was to be rightly understood? It would be disingenuous to suggest the guidance of the Holy Spirit would eliminate all disagreement when "the best and wisest of men generally all disagree respecting them" (*Letters*, p. 183). In Hicks' view, the unfortunate result of those disagreements was too often persecution and war. Stating this in a letter to his neighbor, Phebe Willis, generated a storm of controversy:

> *"The effects produced by the book called the Scriptures… have been the cause of fourfold more harm than good to Christendom since the apostles' days – and which I think must be indubitably plain to every faithful, honest mind that has investigated her history, free from the undue bias of education and tradition." (Letters, p. 54)*

In the same letter, Hicks wrote he believed some of these disputes were the result of intentional deception by those who twisted the verses and mangled their meanings to fit pre-conceived notions - by implication, this included his Quaker critics:

> *"And this is the cause why many turn from him [Jesus] to the teachings of men or books, because they can mostly turn their teachings to suit their own ends. Hence, plain truth is disagreeable to them, but teachings that they can interpret to suit their own inclinations - as most men do with the Scriptures - these they cry up and speak highly of."* (Letters, p. 57)

Bible Addiction

To the evident horror of some of his opponents, on at least one occasion, Hicks proposed a radical (if unlikely) solution - universal scriptural amnesia. When Phebe Willis challenged him on this point, he didn't deny considering the prospect. Perhaps to tweak her, he compared Bible reading to drinking hard liquor and suggested there might be benefits to "drying out":

> *"I might have said that I did not know but it might be as well that they were entirely done away, but never expressed this as my settled belief. But I may add that I sometimes think that if they are really needful and useful to a few who make a right use of them, yet as I believe they are doing great harm to multitudes of others, whether it would not be better for the few, who find some comfort and help from them, to give them up for a time - until the wrong use and abuse of them are done away - in the same manner as (in a moral relation) it might be better for the inhabitants of the world if distillation, and the means of making spirituous liquors, were for a time given up and done away, until the wrong use and abuse of them are done away and forgotten - although it might deprive some of the benefit of them, who use those articles only to their comfort and help. For if after a time it might be thought right to renew the making it - when the intemperate use and abuse was done away - it would be a very easy thing for man to make it again.*
>
> *"Just so, in respect to the Scriptures - it would be a very easy thing for Divine Wisdom and Goodness to raise up and qualify some of his faithful servants to write Scriptures, if he should think best, as good and as competent for the generation in which they lived - and likely would be much better than those written so many hundred years since."* (Letters, p. 96)

Continuing Revelation

From its earliest days, the Society of Friends has held that immediate revelation still occurs - basing this belief on John 16:12-13 ("I have yet many things to say unto you, but ye cannot bear them now. Howbeit when he, the Spirit of truth, is come, he will guide you into all truth: for he shall not speak of himself; but whatsoever he shall hear, that shall he speak: and he will shew you things to come."). But the difficulties of interpreting scripture are minor compared to those involved in establishing the truth of a new revelation. Consider, for example, the Qur'an. Among Muslims, it is unquestionably taken as divine revelation, but after fourteen hundred years, few Christians grant it that status.

Elias Hicks was well aware of the scriptural basis for continuing revelation, and saw in it the promise of revelations tailored to the needs of each succeeding age:

> *"Jesus says, 'I have many things to say unto you, but you cannot bear them now. But when he, the Spirit of Truth comes, he shall lead you and guide you into all truth' – then certainly better than the journals and epistles of men's writing in a previous age, although written by divine inspiration." (Letters, p. 181)*

Scripture & Reason

Claims of new revelations had deep roots among Friends. The topic of the second proposition in Barclay's *Apology* is immediate revelation. In it, Barclay wrote that proof of its truth came when, "Neither scripture nor sound reason will contradict it." Barclay saw these as equally important tests, but over time, many Friends have tended to depend more on one or the other of Barclay's criteria - some upholding reason and downplaying the role of scripture, while others do the opposite.

Hicks privileged reason. Moreover, he was willing to apply reason to the evaluation of the Bible. In a letter to William Poole, he defended testing scripture with reason:

> *"I am established in the sentiment, that truth never loses by close investigation, but rises thereby more bright and clear... "I have often thought, that nothing more sullies and degrades the scriptures of truth, than the fears that many of their advocates manifest, in regard to the investigation of them, and insisting upon their being taken and believed literally just as they are, whether consonant with reason, yea or nay.*

"That book that will not bear the test of all the investigation that the human mind is capable of going into, and still rise superior to all the cavils and false insinuations that may be cast upon it, cannot be of much use to mankind." (Unpublished Letter to William Poole, December 28, 1819)

For Elias Hicks, continuing revelation was essential to the "progress in reformation" required of each generation - i.e., the ongoing work of revealing and building the kingdom of heaven on earth. New revelation will guide humanity to new insights and renewed vitality - but only if people are willing to "press forward."

"Epistles may be written suited to the present time in which they are written. Nevertheless, if the right improvement was made by every generation, new things would be opened in every generation that would supersede what had gone before - just as the gospel superseded the law. Thus, an advancement in reformation would be experienced, old things would be left behind and new things in the wisdom of Truth would be opened on the minds of honest travelers Zion-ward.

"But alas! Instead of pressing forward towards the mark for the prize and high calling of God, how many are looking back to the weak and beggarly elements to which they seem willing to be in bondage?" (Letters, p. 184)

Notice "new things... supersede what had gone before." If the Bible contradicts the immediate guidance of the Light Within, scripture needs to step aside. To his opponents, this was heresy.

Things I Believe But Can't Prove

The Bible is History

Because he was so often questioned, there may be a better record of his beliefs about scripture than any other topic. Even so, there are issues he did not address because they were not topics of interest or controversy in his day. One of interest today is that Elias Hicks was a biblical literalist.

To Hicks, the Bible is history - not myths, legends, and stories that people made up. He believed Adam and Eve were real people; and a great flood wiped out everyone except Noah and his family. Satan, angels, devils, and other spiritual beings existed in the past and still exist.

There is an important difference, however, between Hicks' literalism and that of people today. While he seems to have been aware of some of the biblical scholarship of his day, it was many years after his death before biblical criticism gained prominence or a general audience. Hicks' literalism was naïve - an affirmation of what was generally known and believed - not a denial of years of research and careful analysis. I can only speculate how he would have reacted to later investigations of the Bible - my guess is he would find it fascinating and it would have deepened his appreciation of these works of ancient wisdom.

For Hicks, the mere facts of history are true, but they are not the essence of the scripture. The spiritual meaning of an historical event was frequently veiled to the participants and only revealed years later by the inspiration of the Holy Spirit acting on the mind of a faithful reader. For example, it may be a literal fact that the children of Israel entered the Promised Land after wandering for forty years in the desert, but spiritually, that event may be best understood by a reader as foreshadowing that individual's entrance into heaven after the trials and troubles of his or her earthly sojourn. This is, moreover, not the one true meaning of this outward event. Another reader, faithfully submitting to the Inward Teacher, might be led to a different - and for that reader, true - interpretation of its spiritual import.

Similarly, he trusted that the writers of the Hebrew Scriptures were inspired to write, albeit unknowingly, about Jesus as their future Messiah. In the suffering servant passages, for example, Isaiah may have believed he was writing about the many sufferings of Israel, but for Hicks (as for most Christians of his day) the Holy Spirit had worked on the prophet to interject prophecies of the passion of Christ into this book - prophecies Jesus would fulfill hundreds of years later. Starting with this assumption, in order to truly understand the Hebrew Scriptures, they must be read in light of the Christian scriptures, and that is the way Hicks read them.

Likewise, the Hebrew Testament is, for him, an Old Testament. As stated in Hebrews 8:13, "By calling this covenant 'new', he has made the first one obsolete; and what is obsolete and ageing will soon disappear." Hicks believed Jesus came to fulfill and end the old covenant, so a new covenant (that is, a new testament) could be inaugurated.

The Epistle to the Hebrews

The Bible is a large and complex collection of written materials. It may be inevitable that those who read it regularly will develop favorites. Some, for example, prefer the mystical character of the Gospel of John, while others resonate with the earthier Jesus in the Gospel of Mark. These may be conscious choices, but for many readers, the bias may be hidden even from themselves.

Elias Hicks never identified particular books as favorites, but there are clues as to which he most highly valued and trusted. I believe his reading of scripture was especially influenced by the Epistle to the Hebrews.

In the course of preparing his journal, letters, and essays for publication, I spent a great deal of time ferreting out and identifying the many scriptural quotes and allusions Hicks included in them. I thought I could gain insight into his thinking by examining the passages referenced – in the King James Version he would have used – side-by-side with his words. Doing so gave me a deep appreciation for his grasp of scripture and for the depth of reading it implied. As a former statistician, I also systematically identified most common verses and books, but a numerical answer was unsatisfying – raw counts didn't tell a story – and I let it go.

Little things can sometimes reveal hidden preferences. A favored text can unconsciously influence the reading of other material. I noticed three places in his journal (pp. 234, 235, 284) where Hicks used variations on the phrase "thorns and briars choke the good seed." I assumed these were references to the parable of the sower and the seed – a parable Hicks refers to other times, but the language wasn't exactly right – the gospels mention thorns, but not briars – but I don't think Hicks wrote with a Bible always at hand to reference. It was an interesting anomaly, but I let it go.

As I started work on the material for this book, I had a feeling Hicks was frequently looking to Hebrews, especially to chapter nine. One evening, I read the book, just to see what I would find. When I got to Hebrews 6:8, "But that which beareth thorns and briars is rejected," I stopped to look up the anomalous phrases in the journal. For me, this was a critical clue – the language of Hebrews was so deeply planted in the mind of Elias Hicks that it had leaked into the story of the sower.

This isn't sufficient evidence to make an air-tight case, but it confirmed my intuitions. I believe in Hebrews, Elias Hicks found a key to unlock the rest of the Bible. In particular, he turned to chapter nine, which is bracketed by two retellings of the promise of a new covenant found in chapter thirty-one of the book of Jeremiah – one of the places where Christians see prophecy of a coming Messiah:

"Behold, the days come, saith the LORD, that I will make a new covenant... I will put my law in their inward parts, and write it in their hearts; and will be their God, and they shall be my people. And they shall teach no

more every man his neighbour, and every man his brother, saying, Know the LORD: for they shall all know me, from the least of them unto the greatest of them, saith the LORD: for I will forgive their iniquity, and I will remember their sin no more." (Jeremiah 31:31, 33-34)

Hebrews 8:10-12 and Hebrews 10:16-17 each reiterate this prophecy. Quakers claim this promised covenant has arrived. The outward law has been replaced with a new law written on the heart of each person. I believe these verses served as markers for Elias Hicks. Hebrews is the heart of scripture and what lies between these two verses is the heart of that heart.

The implications of this in trying to understand Elias Hicks are profound. His beliefs have deep roots in scripture and Hebrews informs his reading of the Bible, so all his beliefs are colored by his understanding of Hebrews. This will be most noticeable in how he addressed the divinity of Jesus and the meaning of the crucifixion – two areas, incidentally, in which his opponents considered him to be conspicuously unsound.

Challenges

For many modern liberal Friends, the Bible is a challenge all by itself. They find it far easier to seek out new revelations than to grapple with old revelation. They thereby surrender the scriptures to others who claim to know exactly what they mean. In doing so, they forsake their birthright and forfeit a treasure.

Elias Hicks provides an example of how to challenge scripture with integrity, intellectual honesty, and humility. The hardest of these was to have the humility to surrender completely to the guidance of the Inward Light and follow wherever it would lead him.

There has been nearly two centuries of biblical scholarship since his death, so we start from a very different place than he did. We have advantages he did not, but the same essential questions face us.

Do we have both the daring and the humility to engage, under the direction of the Holy Spirit, with wisdom distilled over thousands of years?

Will we go whichever way the Inward Light points us?

Faithfulness & the Inward Light

"Dwell low in your minds, as it is only in the valley of humiliation that we can have fellowship with the Oppressed Seed." (Letters, p. 23)

Elias Hicks believed God owes humanity nothing, but provides everything anyone has and everything anyone needs. All things, however, are granted in stewardship - not as possessions to be used or misused, abused or discarded as we see fit. They are under our care for a short while and then we will give them up again. Some are enjoyed for a lifetime, others briefly.

"All our rich blessings are but the goods of our kind and gracious Benefactor and are only loaned to us during his good pleasure. So when he calls for them - as they are his just right - we ought cheerfully to surrender them with due acknowledgments and gratitude for the unmerited favor in suffering us to enjoy them so long as we have." (Letters, p. 182)

In his journal (p. 14), he speaks of humanity as "limited, borrowed beings" - recognizing our very being, even our bodies, are ours only temporarily. In the end, each person will have to account for how those loans were managed - what value they produced for their true owner.

Free Will

Of the many precious gifts humanity received, the greatest is free will. Each person has an absolute right to choose what to do with the abilities and material goods granted to her or his care, but in return for all these gifts, each person owes complete and utter obedience to divine direction. Not as a puppet - fidelity is only real when freely chosen and freely given. In 1820, William B. Irish, a non-Quaker who was questioning his faith, exchanged a pair of letters with Hicks, asking for advice. In his first response, Hicks presented his views on the purpose of human life and the importance of free will in achieving that goal:

"I believe that the Almighty Creator of the universe never had but one sole purpose and design in creating man and placing him on this terraqueous globe – and that was to do his will and thereby to continue in a state of happy union and communion with him through the Spirit... but only in his own free and voluntary choice to attend to and do his holy will in all things, and thereby glorify and enjoy him – which all agree to be the chief end and design of man's creation." (Letters, pp. 79-80)

Soon after receiving a reply to his second letter, Irish requested membership in the Religious Society of Friends. His son, born in 1830, was named Elias Hicks Irish.

The Inward Light of Christ

If they are to fulfill this purpose, people need to know what God requires of them. Without some guidance, how could people fulfill their obligation? In 1826, Hicks received a letter from a man advocating for the establishment of a common wealth society (i.e., a community that held all its wealth and material possessions in common). In his answer, Hicks advised the society's adherents to first put their lives under the guidance of the Light Within. Only then would they be able to enter into a true and just commonwealth:

"But did we all as individuals take the Spirit of Truth, or Light Within, as our only rule and guide in all things, we should all then be willing and thereby enabled to do justly, love mercy, and walk humbly with God. Then we should hold all things in common and call nothing our own, but consider all our blessings as only lent to us – to be used and distributed by us in such manner and way as his Holy Spirit, or the Inward Teacher, may from time to time direct. Hence, we should be made all equal, accountable to none but God alone for the right use or abuse of his blessings... And as this order in society becomes established, each individual would be left in the enjoyment and possession of true liberty and independence, and every social obligation be justly and amply fulfilled." (Letters, pp. 209-10)

The Ultimate Rule and Guide

For some, the Bible is held to be the ultimate rule and guide in all things. Others look to specially designated individuals – a priest or minister – to discern God's will and convey it to them. Friends have taken a very different route. From the beginning, Quakers have claimed immediate divine guidance constantly streams into the heart and soul of each person. In a letter to a skeptical neighbor, Elias Hicks asserted his place in that tradition.

> *"George Fox was raised up to bear testimony to the Light and Spirit of Truth in the hearts and consciences of men and women as the only sure rule of faith and practice – both in relation to religious and moral things – and which was complete and sufficient without the aid of books or men." (Letters, p. 55)*

This guide was called by a variety of names. Hicks referred to it as the Light of Christ or Christ the Light, the Holy Spirit or the Inward Teacher, the Light of the Spirit of God, the Inward Light and Law, the Light Within, the Spirit of Truth, and more. Borrowing from George Fox, he wrote, "Christ by his Light and Spirit was come to teach his people himself" (*Journal*, p. 276). Hicks made no distinction between Light, Spirit, and Christ – all referred to the same divine being. The significance was not in the name used, but in the infallible guidance provided.

> *"I was led to call upon Friends to rally to our standard, the Light Within, which is a principle of perfect rectitude and justice, and if rightly attended to, will lead us to withdraw from all kind of conduct and commerce that is in the least degree tinged with injustice and oppression." (Journal, p. 343)*

Moreover, its content is unique to each person. For Hicks, this divine director was what Jesus referred to when he challenged his disciples to "take up the cross daily" (Luke 9:23). In the last letter written before he died, he offered this definition:

> *"Some may query, what is the cross of Christ? To these, I answer, it is the perfect law of God that was written on the tablet of his heart and on the heart of every rational creature in such indelible characters that all the power of mortals cannot erase nor obliterate. Neither is there any other power or means given or dispensed to the children of men, but this Inward Law and Light, by which the true and saving knowledge of God can be obtained. And by this Inward Law and Light, all will be either justified or condemned. And all will be made to know God for themselves and be left without excuse." (Letters, p. 265)*

This "Inward Law" is engraved on "the heart of every rational creature." Divine guidance is universally available – not just to Quakers or to Christians.

Living Faithfully

Individuals aren't called to follow the guidance of the Light of Christ only in "the big things." Everyday life presents an unending series of little opportunities to embrace or to turn away from God. The goal is to choose God deliberately, and to make that habit virtually automatic.

> *"And even when we proceed in his [God's] counsel, and enter into concerns either of a temporal or of a religious nature, he does not leave it for us to judge how long or how far we may proceed therein, but he keeps the reins in his own hand. Like the well-advised husbandman when breaking the horse, that noble and – when well broken by his will being fully subjected – useful and docile quadruped. His first business is to learn him to lead, so as to follow his master cheerfully – contrary to his own will." (Letters, p. 151)*

From his own painful experiences, Hicks knew it is human nature to take the easy way - to do the things that give personal pleasure - rather than choosing submission to the divine will.

> *"Let neither trials, afflictions, nor any other thing that transpires hinder us or turn us aside from that necessary daily labor in surrendering ourselves up fully to the operation of that purifying, cleansing baptism that makes the heart clean from all the dross and tin of our fallen, corrupt natures." (Letters, p. 69)*

This "cleansing baptism" was not, of course, accomplished with water. When Friends used the term, baptism, they were referring to an inward, spiritual event - the baptism "with the Holy Ghost and with fire" from the gospels (Matthew 3:11 and Luke 3:16). Likewise, it was not something that occurred once in a lifetime. Hicks referred in letters and his journal to "deep," "trying," and "excruciating" baptisms - times of trial and testing he endured as part of the ongoing process of working out his salvation "in fear and trembling."

Many of Hicks' greatest trials came when he traveled in the ministry. From a twenty-first-century vantage, it might seem like fun to get off the farm and take a little trip. But the roads were rough and harsh two hundred years ago, the food of indifferent quality, and the beds he slept in - whether at an inn or staying with a family - were likely to be hard, narrow, and often shared with other itinerant men. He frequently wished he was free to return home, but didn't feel released by God to do so:

> *"I hope thy patience will so hold out as not to think the time too long, as it respects my absence from thee, as no doubt, the Lord's time is always the best time, and to know this is my principle care. And I feel abundantly*

> *thankful that thus far I have got along in the clearness, which produces sweet peace of mind – a blessing not to be equaled by any temporal blessing." (Unpublished letter to Jemima Hicks, December 9, 1817)*

More than once, Hicks reflected on twin stories about Moses leading the children of Israel through the Sinai desert. In chapter seventeen of Exodus, the people needed water and God commanded Moses to strike a rock with his staff. When he did, water flowed from the rock. In chapter twenty in the book of Numbers, there is a similar story of thirst and divine intervention, but this time, God tells Moses to speak to the rock. Instead Moses repeats his earlier actions – he strikes the rock and water gushes out. It is a minor act of disobedience, but the punishment for it is dramatic. Moses will be permitted to see the Promised Land, but will never enter it. In considering these stories, Hicks never questioned whether this penalty was just – all God's acts are just – but instead applied the lesson to himself:

> *"Sometimes we are commanded to smite the rock and sometimes, only to speak to it. And we have nothing to do but to mind our leader and obey the word of command… when he says, 'Smite the rock,' smite it. And when he says withhold, always obey. And then it will go well with us – let others do as they will. And he will lead us in the way everlasting." (Letters, pp. 113-114)*

Challenges

This chapter began with a quote about being "in the valley of humiliation." This was at the core of Hicks' sense of what it means to be faithful – to freely enter the valley of humiliation. He strove to live always in that valley.

His use of the word "humiliation" should not be taken as a sanction for belittling others. To Hicks, humiliation is humbling oneself. Faithfulness comes when a person is willing to take up the daily cross she or he is asked to bear – to answer God's hopes and dreams written in the heart, rather than one's own.

Are we prepared to give up our hopes and dreams if the Spirit of Truth calls us elsewhere?

God

"It is perfectly consistent with truth, and the reason and nature of things, that as God is the only good, so he never does nor can – according to his own unchangeable nature and essence – command or ordain any other than good works for his rational children to walk in." (Letters, p. 227)

With the exception of his views on Jesus (addressed in the next chapter), Elias Hicks held fairly conventional beliefs about God for a Quaker of his times. Friends believed God to be an invisible, eternal Spirit, whose desires for each person could be known directly by the movements of the Inward Light within every heart and soul. All outward sources, including the Bible, were seen as poor substitutes for this immediate experience. Hicks spoke for many Friends when in 1828, he wrote:

"Not all the books ever written, nor all the external miracles recorded in the Scriptures, nor all other external evidence of what kind soever, has ever revealed God (who is an eternal, invisible Spirit) to any one of the children of men." (Letters, p. 225)

God is only truly revealed directly and spiritually. Not only does the Light Within open a channel with the divine, but its communications are in a form that allows them to be clearly understood by the human mind.

"For when we consider that the infinitely wise and perfect God, in creation has seen fit to make man a rational being, hence, all his communications and revelations to him must and will be rational, and in a way to be rationally understood." (Letters, p. 226)

God, in other words, is always available and always dependable.

The Essential Unity of God

Elias Hicks joined early Friends in rejecting Trinitarian doctrine. Like them, he unquestioningly held to the essential monotheism expressed in scripture, while at the same time, never doubting God comes in different guises. The scriptural basis of this unity was clearly spelled out in an 1820 letter to his closest friend, William Poole:

"As to the unchangeable unity of the Divine Power and great first cause of all created existence, as declared to Moses, viz., 'I am that I am.' [Exodus 3:14] We must believe [God] is incapable of divisibility, for as there can be but one will in heaven to render it a place of perfect happiness, so there can be but one will in God, who is the king, immortal, invisible [1 Timothy 1:17], whose dwelling is in the Light, that no mortal can approach [1 Timothy 6:16], and who saith by his prophet, Isaiah, 'Who hath told it from that time? Have not I, the Lord? And there is no God else beside me, a just God and a Savior. There is none beside me. Look unto me and be ye saved all the ends of the earth, for I am God and there is none else.' [Isaiah 45:21-22]" (Letters, p. 100)

Trinitarian Doctrine

Trinitarian doctrine states there are three "persons" in one God. It is an explanation of the triune God first proposed in the early third century by Tertullian and adopted by a church council in the year 325. Hicks' arguments against the doctrine closely followed those William Penn laid out in his 1668 pamphlet, *The Sandy Foundation Shaken.*[1] His first argument was simply that the word "trinity" is not found in the Bible. On the other hand, a variety of names are used in scripture for the divine. Hicks accepted that all referred to the same God - an undividable unity, present equally everywhere - but he had no use for an abstract and complex theory to explain how this could be accomplished. Hicks gave his assessment of it in a letter to William B. Irish:

"The doctrine of the trinity, as held by many professing Christians, I also consider a weak and vulgar error - that of three distinct persons in one God, and that each of these persons are whole God... as I believe there cannot be a greater absurdity than to apply personality to God in any right sense of the word, as personality implies locality, which signifies limited to place, which would be very impious to say of the infinite Jehovah... There is nothing more plainly nor more fully impressed upon the Israelites by their great lawgiver than to acknowledge but one God. And although they often asserted that the Spirit of the Lord came to them or was upon them, yet they manifest no idea of any divisibility or distinction of person between God and his Spirit - but wherever the Holy Spirit of God is, there is God, and where God is, there is the Holy Spirit." (Letters, pp. 81-82)

---

[1] See Buckley, Paul (Ed.), *Twenty-First Century Penn.* Richmond, Indiana: Earlham School of Religion Publications, 2003, pp. 1-41 for a modern English version.

How can God be One, while still being Father, Son, and Holy Spirit? For many early Friends, the answer was a simple one. In the King James Version of the Bible, the First Epistle of John 5:7 says, "There are three that bear record in heaven, the Father, the Word, and the Holy Ghost: and these three are one." The epistle's author didn't provide an explanation of how this could be and there was no obligation for his readers to make one up. It just is. On this basis, they rejected Trinitarian doctrine as something that theologians "made up," while still accepting that there are three and the three are One.

Hicks had a somewhat more nuanced approach. First, he questioned the accuracy of 1 John 5:7. Also in the letter to William B. Irish, he wrote:

> *"For although the apostle is made to say (agreeable to our present translation) that, 'There are three that bear record in heaven,' yet he assures us that, 'these three are but one.' And we have no certainty that they have given us the apostle's sense clearly, as we have no reason to believe that the translators were inspired men."* (Letters, p. 81)

Even in the early nineteenth century, there were Bible scholars who doubted the veracity of this translation and modern translations of that verse are very different. In the New International Version, verses seven and eight read, "For there are three that testify: the Spirit, the water and the blood; and the three are in agreement." Hicks was right to doubt – perhaps because he had read some of the scholarship and perhaps (as Quakers are prone to claim) from direct divine inspiration.

In a letter arguing against the need for water in baptism to Benjamin Ferris (who would become the first clerk of the Hicksite Philadelphia Yearly Meeting), he quoted from Matthew 28:19, one of two Bible verses that refer to Father, Son, and Holy Ghost, but is again clearly emphasizing the unity of God:

> *"And there is another conclusive argument [which] arises from the tenor of the command of Jesus to his disciples as recorded by Matthew in his 28th chapter, 'Go ye therefore and teach all nations, baptizing them into' (for so it ought to be rendered) 'the name of the Father, and of the Son, and of the Holy Ghost.' Therefore, as these three make but one Power and one Spirit – for God is one Spirit and his name One, being his Power – I again aver no man ever did nor ever can baptize any person with material water into the name of Father, Son, and Holy Ghost."* (Letters, p. 129)

In short, Elias Hicks believed there was but one God; albeit a God who was called by different names at different times. This position can and did lead to charges he was a Unitarian. This accusation will be addressed in the next chapter, *Jesus.*

God's Power

Elias Hicks believed God is all-powerful and all-good, but if God's beneficence and omnipotence are both assumed, questions about evil naturally arise. Where does evil come from? And why doesn't God act to prevent it? Why, for example, doesn't God act to prevent the death of an innocent? Hicks' answer was simple: God's ways are not our ways. He may not have understood why some things happened, but was unshakably sure that all God's actions were right and just.

> *"I consider it impossible that a pure, just, and holy God could ever act arbitrarily, oppressively, or tyrannically towards his rational creation. Nevertheless, I believe that God, who is the author and preserver of all created existence, may and sometimes does act in a way so far beyond the investigation of finite man in his fallen state that in the darkness he is enveloped in, he accuses him of acting arbitrarily and oppressively." (Letters, p. 187)*

Limits on God

Nevertheless, Hicks believed God was not free to do anything. Divine nature could not be negated - God could only act in accordance with God's essential character. By this standard, divine goodness restrains the use of divine power.

> *"There is an overruling and gracious Providence, not bound entirely by any general laws, but is always free and at liberty to act... but always in conformity to his justice, mercy, and truth." (Letters, p. 188)*

This still does not explain the existence of evil. Why would the Creator fashion a world in which injustice, cruelty, and deceit are so common? Couldn't creation have been pre-planned so righteousness always prevailed? Theories of predestination make this assumption - whatever happens was pre-ordained and must be God's will, including the evil deeds people commit. Hicks was familiar with this argument - it had been central to debates William Penn engaged in with Presbyterians in the middle of the seventeenth century - and Hicks utterly rejected it:

> *"The doctrine of predestination and election, with many other erroneous opinions, have their source in erroneous ideas and views that most people have formed of the Divine Character - especially as it regards his agency*

and power. For as he is acknowledged to be almighty, and all things possible with God, most people in this unlimited view think he can do any and every thing… and his doing of it, makes it right." (Letters, p. 90)

God is inherently righteous and by nature, cannot act otherwise. Beyond these intrinsic limits, God has self-limited by the gift of free will. Granting humanity the ability to choose without restraint meant individuals had the ability to introduce evil into the world. This choice carried with it the risk that a person's salvation could be earned or lost. Anything less would make a mockery of free will - people would have the appearance of freedom and even believe they could act as they pleased, but their ultimate choice would be a sham. To Hicks, predestination would encumber God with different, but equally inconsistent, obligations - to inflict salvation on unwilling sinners and to justify the unjust.

"As a Friend of high standing once argued with me in regard to his [God's] power to save all mankind - that if it was agreeable to his pleasure, he could convert and save all mankind in a moment. To which I objected the impossibility of any power in heaven or in earth saving any rational immortal soul - by an act of mere coercion or power - that had in its own will and choice fallen into a state of death and condemnation. For if he could - contrary to the choice and will of one immortal soul that had fallen by transgression - restore it again by a mere act of power against the will of the creature, then I have no doubt but all will be saved, because perfect justice could not (consistent with its own nature) save one and reject another - as all are by him considered in one predicament, that is, in a state of unbelief, that he might alike have mercy upon all." (Letters, p. 90)

By allowing human freedom, a related divine handicap was self-imposed: God cannot see into the future. Human choices change the course of creation.

"When I mentioned infinite prescience, I was far from considering the term infinite to comprehend an entire foreknowledge of every event that should transpire through all the endless ages of futurity. This view has its origin in the dark and inconsistent doctrine of foreordination and hath no foundation in truth, nor in the reason and nature of things - as the term infinite implies no such thing, but merely a power and prescience that is unbounded by any other being or power. This interpretation is justified by Jehovah, when he said, 'It repenteth me that I have made man on the earth,' [Genesis 6:6] when he [humanity] had corrupted his ways. But this he

could not have said, if he had foreknown all that came to pass after his creation." (Letters, p. 189)

In summary, Hicks understood God to be so powerful as to allow God to be powerless. Of the divine attributes, love trumps all others; and out of that love, God gave humanity free will and with it, the ability to disappoint or to serve faithfully.

Things I Believe But Can't Prove

As mentioned above, Elias Hicks never felt the need to explain how he reconciled the unity of God with the multiplicity of names for God - especially for the three most Christians see as the names of the three separate persons of the Trinity: Father, Son, and Holy Spirit. If the inspired writers of the Bible felt no need to explain it, neither did he. More to the point, he saw no need for the intricate doctrinal explanations constructed by theologians centuries after the scriptures were written.

In addition to Father, Son, and Holy Spirit, Hicks had an extensive list of names he used to refer to God: Creator, Providence, Jesus, Christ, Christ the Light, Inward Light, Light of Christ, the Inward Teacher, the Light of the Spirit of God, the Inward Light and Law, the Light Within, the Spirit of Truth, etc. - and he used them interchangeably. None was deemed to identify different "offices," tasks, or roles. All designated the same divine being with the same powers, the same authority, and the same nature.

Modalism

Functionally, Hicks seems to have been a modalist, that is, someone who believes there is one God who becomes manifest to humans in different ways (i.e., different modes) at different times, according to the spiritual needs of each individual. Sometimes, for example, what a person needs is a divine parent and God is present for that person as a heavenly Mother or Father. Other times, people need to feel God truly understands what it means to be human - to be frail, tempted, and suffering. For them, experiencing the presence of God as Jesus is comforting. Likewise, people often feel a need for the Paraclete - a divine helper or advocate, and another name for the Holy Spirit. God is each and God is all.

For a modalist, it is always the same God. Many people - Christian and non-Christian alike - interact with a variety of divine manifestations, all at the same time, and use a multiplicity of names to describe the reality they are experiencing, but God is always One. Only the human perceptions and the human descriptions of that one Divine Being differ.

Modalism (or Sabellianism) has been proposed as an explanation of the triune God for hundreds of years and has been condemned by Christians as a heresy for nearly as long. Although it may not have originated with him, it is named for the third century theologian, Sabellius, who was excommunicated for preaching it in the year 220. Some early Friends, including George Fox and William Penn, use similar language in their descriptions of God.

This in no way substantiates claims that Hicks denied the divinity of Jesus or that he was a Unitarian. Clearly he was not, but just as clearly, he was not a conventional Trinitarian.

Jesus

"The three principal requisites to the being and well-being of a Christian...
The first being a real belief in God and Christ as one undivided essence -
known and believed in, inwardly and spiritually."
(Journal, p. 349)

Two of the most serious charges against Elias Hicks were that he denied Jesus' divinity and virgin birth - accusations he unequivocally denied, although to no effect. The bases of these allegations can be found in the ambiguity of Hicks' own words. His beliefs were decidedly unorthodox, although not in the ways his opponents thought they were. In fact, had his adversaries listened a little more carefully and understood more clearly what he actually believed, they may have found his true beliefs even more unsettling.

Hicks delved deeply into the Bible - especially the Epistle to the Hebrews - in attempting to understand what scripture says about both the human and divine natures of Jesus. In addition to scriptural exploration, he applied a strong dose of rational reasoning to the task. The result was a nuanced and unconventional view of who Jesus was, how he relates to God the Father, and what his mission was during his time on earth.

Not Trinitarian & Not Unitarian

In the last chapter, the traditional Quaker rejection of Trinitarianism was discussed. Hicks joined in dismissing that doctrine, but at least some of his opponents did not - considering it to be at the core of a Christian faith. In addition, they seemed to feel anyone who was not a Trinitarian must be a Unitarian and therefore, must deny the divinity of Jesus. Although Hicks emphatically denied he was a Unitarian, they were never convinced.

The Nature of the Old and New Covenants

To appreciate what Elias Hicks believed about Jesus requires a clear understanding of, and a careful distinction between, the Old (or Jewish) and New (or Christian) Covenants. The Mosaic Law was, in Hicks' view, "an outward covenant" with "all open to the view of the external senses of men and women." In an 1825 letter to his good friend, William Poole, Hicks enumerates some of its essential aspects:

> *"The Jewish Covenant and Law was outward and external, and all its usefulness as to its effects was outward and external – an outward salvation, an outward heaven and land of rest, an outward religion, outward priesthood, outward sacrifices, outward atoning, offerings, and oblations. And this outward covenant with all its parts, was established and sealed by outward miracles – not reported to that people as having been done in a distant country at a time long before they existed – for such reports they would not have believed. It would have been no evidence to them, they would have considered it mere hearsay. They would have required proof of their certainty which nothing could give them but working the miracles in their presence, that they might see and behold them self-evidently by their external senses, and no other miracles would they believe." (Unpublished Letter to William Poole, May 4, 1825)*

While the old covenant had been based on outward (i.e., physical and observable) rituals and practices, the new covenant instituted by Jesus was *entirely* inward (i.e., spiritual and not visible to the senses). In another letter to Poole, Hicks explained:

> *"But in and under the gospel dispensation, the law and covenant is spiritual and universal – written in the heart of every rational being under heaven – and is therefore invisible to all the external senses and is only manifested by its fruits. And as the law and covenant are spiritual and internal, so likewise, the Messiah and Comforter of the gospel dispensation are spiritual, and only internally and spiritually known and manifested – and is universally manifested to all the children of men the world over, and by whom the gospel is preached in every rational creature." (Letters, p. 102)*

The new covenant is defined as universal – it encompasses all of humanity – whereas the old covenant had been particular to the Jews. Hicks saw the two covenants as fundamentally distinct: old/new, outward/inward, particular/universal, physical/spiritual.

Moreover, as described in Hebrews 10:1 ("The law is only a shadow of the good things that are coming – not the realities themselves"), outward actions ("shadows") prefigured inward "substance." This means the ultimate significance of an event in the Old Testament may not be apparent when it occurred, only becoming clear when the corresponding inward substance is revealed in the New Testament.

The Meaning of Miracles

These differences between the old and new covenants are important in considering the purposes and significance of miracles. As outward events, to Hicks they could only be identified with the old covenant. They were physical evidence for people who could only accept an outward proof. Christians have direct access to the divine through the Inward Light and, therefore, have no need for such external evidence.

> *"All the external miracles of the Jewish covenant had but one aim and end... to prove to that dark and ignorant people (debased by their bondage) that there was a living and invisible God... Hence, the reason likewise of the many miracles that Jesus was empowered to work among them, as they were too outward and carnal to receive evidence through any other medium. And we likewise see that none but those who believed on him as their promised Messiah were prepared to receive and obey his last counsel and command, to turn from outward and external evidence to that which is inward and spiritual... For when Moses is read – or the law state with outward miracles – there is a veil upon the heart and it leads back to the letter or external evidence which killeth. But this veil is taken away in Christ – or the gospel state – wherein all have free access to the Throne of Grace without priest or book." (Letters, p. 215)*

Hicks felt that when Christians asserted miracles were evidence of God acting in the world, they were backsliding – not living up to the standards of the new covenant, but acting as if they still lived under the old one. More to the point, people in the Old Testament weren't as gullible as that. To them, the report of a miracle that took place out of their sight was no miracle at all. It was "mere hearsay."

> *"For had Moses told Pharaoh and the Israelites... that when he was in the wilderness... he cast his rod on the ground and it became a frightful serpent, and when he was commanded to take it up again, it became a rod in his hand... would they not have been fools to believe him had he not wrought the same miracle in their sight? Hence we learn that the hear-tell of an outward miracle is no miracle to us, and of course, is no sufficient*

evidence to the real truth of any proposition unless supported by some better evidence." (Letters, p. 176)

What especially drew the ire of Hicks' opponents was that, rather than taking miracles as evidence for the divinity of Jesus, Hicks saw them as a demonstrating dependency. In a letter to Poole, he alluded to John 14:10 ("I speak not of myself: but the Father that dwelleth in me, he doeth the works"):

"So Jesus Christ in his outward manifestation was more blest and abundantly more glorified than any other man, and was above all, and therefore was the representation of a God on earth – visible to the external senses – although the power by which he did all his mighty works was the invisible power of God, conferred upon him for that end – he being the instrument through whom God by his power wrought all those mighty works that declared him to be the Son of God with power." (Letters, p. 107)

The Virgin Birth

As mentioned above, Hicks was accused of denying the virgin birth of Jesus. Some of what he said seems to support that charge. He noted, for example, the opening of the gospel of Matthew is "the book of the generation of Jesus, the son of David." It runs from Abraham to Joseph, "the husband of Mary, of whom was born Jesus, who is called Christ" (Matthew 1:16). But this is the genealogy of Jesus - proving Jesus was a descendant of David - only if Jesus was the son of the last person listed, Joseph. Commenting on the virgin birth, Hicks referred to this genealogy and offered the opinion that it showed there was "as much plain Scripture against it as there was for it." (*Letters*, pp. 158)

Nevertheless, he wrote, he accepted the virgin birth of Jesus as true because such an event would be appropriate and useful to people living under the old covenant. Within that context, Hicks interpreted the virgin birth as an outward sign - a miracle performed for the benefit of the people alive then, not those living under the new covenant. In a letter to Gideon Seaman, a neighbor who had questioned him on this point, Hicks added:

"I considered it suited to that dispensation in which outward miracles were their highest evidence...

"If that miraculous birth – as to the miracle itself – was to be of any use to mankind, surely it must have been intended as such to the commonality of Israel in preference to all others. There, it was transacted – and there and

then was the only right time to prove its authenticity, and as a help to prove that Jesus was their promised Messiah." (Letters, pp. 157, 159)

Even so great a miracle was merely an outward event and, therefore, of no value to those who live under the new, inward covenant. Its purpose was to convince people living in the first century. It is inconsequential for Christians living in the nineteenth (or the twenty-first) century.

To the dismay of his opponents, Hicks dismissed the whole issue as ultimately unimportant. Belief or disbelief in the truth of the virgin birth, he said, was not and could not be essential for salvation. If it were, God would surely have provided clear knowledge of it to everyone:

"A belief therein was not an essential to salvation, for that, that is essential to the salvation of the souls of the children of men, is certainly dispensed by our common Creator, to every rational Creature under Heaven, for he is unchangeably perfect, equal in all his ways, and righteous in all his works, and will do equal justice to all, so that all who disobey his manifested will, is left without excuse, for should he manifest any certain thing to a small portion of mankind, as an essential to salvation, and keep it Secret from the greater part, would it not be partial, seeing he is all wise and all powerful, and could as easily manifest it to all as to one." (Unpublished Letter to William Poole, May 4, 1825)

In summary, to Hicks, whether or not Joseph was Jesus' father is of no importance, but Jesus' nature when he was born is crucial.

Jesus' Two Missions

Jesus doesn't just sit on the boundary between the old and new covenants. Jesus is the boundary. For Hicks, that meant Jesus had two distinct, but necessarily related missions. First, as described in Luke 24:44 and Romans 10:4, he was sent to fulfill and end the old covenant:

"Christ coming in the flesh, he had fulfilled the law of Moses relating to the religion and worship of that dispensation, which stood in mere legal righteousness, consisting of mere carnal ordinances, and relating only to the outward or animal body... And that all these were ended and abrogated by the sacrifice of Christ's body on the cross, and whereby he fulfilled all the righteousness of that dispensation... and finished transgression and put an end to all the legal sins of that covenant." (Journal, pp. 265-66)

Having fulfilled the old covenant, Jesus established the new, inward, and everlasting covenant. For Hicks, accomplishing this gospel mission required an essential change in Jesus' nature.

> *"So Jesus, being faithful to the leading of the Spirit of God, fulfilled all the righteousness of the Jewish law and was then prepared to receive additional power from on high, by which he was qualified to enter upon his Gospel mission, and introduce the new covenant."* (Letters, p. 214)

Adoptionism

In the King James Version of the Bible, Hebrews 8:7 reads, "For if that first covenant had been faultless, then should no place have been sought for the second." In other words, the new covenant was only necessary because the Jews had not been faithful in following the requirements of the Law. This was the basis of Jesus first earthly mission - to live "faultless" under the requirements of "that first covenant."

Hicks reasoned that if a divine being fulfilled the requirements of the Law, it was worthless as an example to the Jews. They could excuse themselves by saying the Law was too difficult for a mere human being to follow it faultlessly. They could even charge God with being unfair in asking them to do so. Hicks put this in plain words in a letter to his trusted friend, William Poole in 1821:

> *"He [Jesus] was likewise a real and true man – as the Scriptures abundantly assure us – being the son or offspring of Abraham and David after the flesh, born of an Israelitish virgin, brought up and nursed by his parents and was subject unto them like other children until he arrived to the state of manhood, complying faithfully with all the requisitions and ordinances of the Jewish law – by which he justified his Heavenly Father in giving them that law and commandments. Proving by his faithfully fulfilling all of them, that it was within the capacity and power of every Israelite to have done the same, had they faithfully improved (as he had done) the ability they had received for that end, and by which he condemned their unfaithfulness."* (Letters, p. 108)

Jesus proved "every Israelite" could have been equally faithful; but only if Jesus was solely human. He had to meet all the obligations of the Law using only "the ability they had received." Otherwise, the Jews had not fallen short. He had to be an ordinary man, "tempted like as we are, yet without sin" (Hebrews 4:15), because, if Jesus was divine, fulfilling the laws and commandments would not have "condemned their unfaithfulness" or "justified his Heavenly Father."

This appears to completely vindicate Hicks' opponents. He clearly denied Jesus' divinity *when he was born.* But Hicks believed everything changed when the first mission was accomplished and the second begun.

Transformation in the Jordan River

Hicks identified Jesus' submission to water baptism by John the Baptist as the final requirement of the old covenant. When this was completed, the gospels tell that the Holy Spirit descended on him in the form of a dove and the voice of God declared, "This is my beloved son." Hicks saw this as a moment of transformation. As Jesus came up out of the Jordan River, he received the additional power he needed to declare the good news of the new covenant:

> *"No doubt his soul, when it entered the body prepared for it, was furnished with such a portion of the Divine Spirit as was most consistent with the will of his Heavenly Father, and by which he was enabled to fulfill all the righteousness of the law and covenant given to Israel by Moses and therefore, in a certain sense, might be considered a son of God – as much so as that dispensation would admit of. But if he had been completely so before the baptism of John and the descent of the Holy Ghost, why was that superadded? And why did not his Heavenly Father previous to that time declare him his son in whom he was well pleased?*
>
> *"And when we farther consider that we don't hear anything of him after he was grown to man's estate – not even so much as being tempted – until the Holy Spirit descended upon him, and by which he was then more fully the Son of God, and filled with the divine nature of his Heavenly Father, and thereby qualified to meet the temptations that assailed him. And when he had vanquished temptation, we then find him entering upon his gospel mission and not before." (Letters, pp. 167-68)*

To be clear, according to Hicks, Jesus was adopted as the son of God and thus he became fully divine. In at least one way, however, his divinity is different from that of the Father. God is self-existent, but as an adopted son, Jesus' divinity is derived. Hicks laid this explanation out in a letter in 1827, finishing it by quoting Romans 8:14. By doing so, he affirmed that others could also be adopted:

> *"As to the divinity of Jesus Christ, the son of the virgin, when he arrived to a full state of Sonship in the spiritual generation, he was wholly swallowed up into the divinity of his Heavenly Father, and was one with his Father, with only this difference – his Father's divinity was underived, being self-existent. But the Son's divinity [is] altogether derived from the Father...*

[after baptism Jesus] witnessed the fullness of the second birth, being now born into the nature, spirit, and likeness of his heavenly Father. And God gave witness of it to John [the Baptist], saying, 'This is my beloved son in whom I am well pleased.' And this agrees with Paul's testimony when he assures us that, 'As many as are led by the Spirit of God, they are the sons of God.'" (Letters, p. 214)

In an earlier letter to William Poole, Hicks had referred to another verse in the Epistle to the Romans (8:17), similarly suggesting that others, by their faithfulness, could become divine in the same way:

"Jesus did all in the outward by the power of his Heavenly Father [John 14:10]... God was in Christ, even in that very man called Jesus of Nazareth, and through him as a proper vehicle wrought all those mighty works... And so far as that holy man, Jesus, was a partaker of the divine nature of his Heavenly Father, so far also was he divine. And so far likewise as he is in any other of his children born anew by his Spirit, and they become partakers of his divine nature, they are likewise divine. And as Paul says, these are heirs of God, and joint heirs with Christ Jesus." (Letters, p. 103)

Elias Hicks does not deny the divinity of Jesus, but what he means by it is something quite different from the orthodox view. Jesus was born an extraordinary man, but just a man. He achieved a state of utter faithfulness to the demands of the Law that others had not, and was subsequently taken into God and adopted as a son of God. With this additional gift of power, he was able to do things no other human had done and inaugurated a new relationship between God and humanity.

The Crucifixion

Coming up out of the Jordan, Jesus embarked on this second mission. As a consequence of his work in instituting a new covenant, Jesus was crucified. For most Christians, this is why Jesus was born - so that he would be crucified. This marks another point of departure for Hicks. He considered this belief to be a slander on God. Any being who would create a creature for the express purpose of having it cruelly tortured and executed would be a monster, not God. Moreover, in dying for his faithfulness, Jesus was not unique - there have been many martyrs throughout the ages. All were killed because they chose to die faithfully, rather than to deny God and live.

As recorded in the gospels, Jesus' death was the unjust act of wicked people - as have been the deaths of so many others. If God had intended Jesus to be crucified, those wicked people would have been doing what God wanted them to do, and therefore their actions would have been justified. Far from being God's will, Jesus' death, like the deaths of all the prophets and martyrs, was a supreme act of faithfulness.

> *"For if it was the purpose and will of God that he [Jesus] should die by the hands of wicked men, then the Jews, by crucifying him, would have done God's will, and of course, would all have stood justified in his sight - which could not be. But it was permitted so to be, as it had been with many of the prophets and wise and good men that were before him, who suffered death by the hands of wicked men for righteousness sake, as examples to those that came after, that they should account nothing too dear to give up for the Truth's sake, not even their own lives."* (Letters, p. 170)

The Meaning of the Crucifixion

Jesus' death was not, however, exactly the same as the deaths of the other martyrs. Most Christians would say Jesus died to save them, but Hicks saw a different reason given in the Epistle to the Hebrews. According to Hebrews 9:15, he died "for the redemption of the transgressions that were under the first testament," in other words, for sins committed under the Mosaic Law. This is a major theme in Hebrews - that Jesus offered a blood sacrifice which ended the need for all such outward rites. It was the final ritual - the capstone of the old covenant.

> *"I do not consider that the crucifixion of the outward body of flesh and blood of Jesus on the cross was an atonement for any sins but the legal sins of the Jews - for as their law was outward, so their legal sins and their penalties were outward. And these could be atoned for by an outward sacrifice."* (Letters, p. 171)

As mentioned above, some outward events are shadows that prefigure an inward substance. Hicks saw the crucifixion as foreshadowing the inward salvation that people experience under the new covenant.

> *"And this last outward sacrifice was a full type of the inward sacrifice that every sinner must make in giving up that sinful life of his own will - in and by which he hath from time to time crucified the innocent life of God in his own soul, and which Paul calls 'the old man with his deeds,' or 'the man of sin and son of perdition,' who hath taken God's seat in the heart, and there exalteth itself above all that is called God or is worshipped - sitting as Judge and Supreme."* (Letters, p. 171)

In other words, Jesus died outwardly to prefigure the way in which each person must inwardly die to sin and be born fresh as a child of God.

Resurrection & Ascension

By the same logic, the outward resurrection and ascension of Jesus are shadows of the rebirth that then can take place within an individual who has surrendered his or her will to God:

> *"And to complete the figure of our redemption, it [the body of Jesus] was raised again outwardly... And his outward ascension, as it was manifest to the external senses of his disciples, must be the appearance of the outward man – as the immortal spirit of the Savior never was nor never could be seen by the outward eyes. Hence this outward ascension was a complete type of the inward or spiritual ascension of the immortal soul of man from an earthly to a heavenly state – by which it regains paradise – and which must and will be regained by every redeemed soul on this side the grave." (Letters, p. 109)*

Things I Believe But Can't Prove

Early Friends tended to spiritualize Jesus - even conflating Jesus with the Inward Light of Christ - but for Hicks, Jesus was very much an embodied human being.

Elias Hicks had unique insight into the life Jesus led during the public ministry recorded in the gospels. Hicks knew what it felt like to be bone-tired from a long journey over poor roads in lousy weather, and to face a hostile audience, and to be openly and widely attacked - by those who were considered religious leaders - as a fraud. This experience was part of the daily cross Elias Hicks willingly bore. This commonality with Jesus as an outward, physical human being gave him a particular relationship with the risen Christ as an inward manifestation of the divine.

They were literally fellow travelers.

Salvation

"I was led to show to Friends... that it was not enough to be delivered from our former sins... unless they also came to witness a complete death to their own wills, so as to be entirely submissive to the will of our Heavenly Father." (Journal, pp. 292-293)

Humanity's Purpose

In Elias Hicks' view, humanity's relationship with God started with the understanding that human beings are creatures who have no existence separate from their Creator. All people are endowed with free will, a gift divinely granted so they can, of their own volition, choose to seek, to find, and to do what God hopes for and desires of them - what is traditionally called God's will. In this way, they can gain salvation.

> *"I believe that the Almighty Creator of the universe never had but one sole purpose and design in creating man and placing him on this terraqueous globe - and that was to do his will and thereby to continue in a state of happy union and communion with him through the Spirit... to give the rational, intelligent creature, man, a fit opportunity to rise above that innocent state in which he was created to the exalted state of virtue and glory, by a just and righteous improvement of the liberty and power conferred upon him by his Gracious Creator for that purpose, and that purpose only, agreeable to the instruction of Divine Wisdom." (Letters, p. 79)*

Hicks believed in sin and redemption. Death marks a transition from an earthly existence to life eternal in either heaven or hell. Each person is free to choose to be faithful or to sin, and so deserves the rewards or punishments she or he receives in the end.

In some ways, these beliefs contradicted those of many Christians and some Quakers of the time.

The Universal Guidance of Inward Light

The first point of departure was in his conviction - shared with other Friends - that God visited each person with perfect guidance by way of the Inward Light and "by this Inward Light only, we are prepared for an admittance into the heavenly kingdom when done with time" (*Journal*, p. 130). All anyone required for salvation was to faithfully attend to its leadings.

Like other Friends, he believed this blessing was not exclusively reserved for Quakers or for Christians or for any other subset of humanity. Everyone - even those who had never heard of Jesus or those, like Jews and Muslims, who knew his name, but denied he was the Son of God - was equally equipped. For it to be otherwise, would require God to be unfair, giving essential help to some but denying it to others. This meant no book - not even the Bible - no teaching or preaching, nor any human minister could be essential for salvation. No one would be condemned merely for lack of an opportunity. The guidance of the Inward Light is provided to everyone.

But only the opportunity to be redeemed is universal, salvation itself is not. In an 1818 letter to Phebe Willis, a close neighbor and frequent critic, Hicks spelled out this belief in a salvation offered to all without exception:

> *"Every one who believes in the existence of God attributes to him justice, mercy, and love, and that he is unchangeable in his nature, and incapable of partiality. Hence he must - and no doubt has - given to every man and woman a complete and sufficient rule of faith and practice without the aid of books or men. And [God] hath so ordered, in the course of events, that the more strictly and faithfully every man and woman lives up to the guidance and teaching of this Inward Anointing - and never turns aside to the right hand or left for the precepts and traditions of men - the more instruction and help they afford one another. And to suppose a written rule to be necessary or much useful is to impeach the divine character, and charge the infinite Jehovah with partiality and injustice, as the greater part of his rational creation has never been furnished with those means. And had they been needful, he certainly would - in order to deal with an even hand of justice - [have] furnished all his rational creatures with them, as it was equally in his power so to have done from the beginning." (Letters, p. 56)*

Free Will

As was discussed above, the key assumption was that God had granted everyone free will, and by doing so, made all accountable for their fates. When people choose to sin, they have no one to blame but themselves. But as long as they live, no one is finally condemned for their bad decisions - the chance to turn to or to re-turn to the Light of Truth always remains. As Hicks wrote to William Poole:

"All man's defilement arises from his own acts – by making a wrong use of his liberty while endued with sufficient power and understanding to have stood, had he made a right use thereof. So this power and ability is continued to him for to enable and lead him in the way of return during the time of his probation." (Letters, p. 120)

Salvation is an ongoing activity, not a one-time thing. Just as the offer of salvation is always present, so is the risk of failure. Deliverance requires constant attention to the leadings of the Light Within.

"Therefore, to this Light and Law in thy heart, I must still recommend thee as the one thing needful and that by which thou canst only be enabled to begin the work of thy salvation. And this alone can only qualify thee to carry it on and finally assist thee to lay the top-stone thereof. But the work is great and gradual, therefore it requires time, patience, and perseverance." (Letters, p. 6)

Sin is Overindulging in Natural Propensities

In the wake of the Great Separations, Charles Stokes, a professionally accomplished and successful Friend from New Jersey, sent Elias Hicks a letter containing a series of questions. Among his answers, Hicks addressed salvation and the source of sin.

No one, he wrote, was predestined to heaven or hell. Nor were any predisposed to iniquity. Neither can any blame the devil. Sin is simply a human choice to overindulge natural, human desires beyond what is proper and necessary for life.

"I should suppose that every man of common understanding, by a proper introversion into himself, would immediately discover that he was never tempted to any evil, but though one or other of the propensities and desires of his common nature as an accountable being. And that those propensities and desires – while kept under the discipline of the cross of Christ, which is God's law written, as the Scriptures declare, on the tablets of our hearts – were all ministers of good to man and qualified him rightly to answer the

end of his creation. For without those propensities and desires, man would be a dormant, inactive creature, as he would have nothing to excite him to action to procure those things necessary to preserve his life, or to seek after an attainment in true knowledge sufficient to introduce him into the knowledge of his Creator and prepare him to be a communicant with him in the realms of blessedness when done with time here on earth." (Letters, pp. 258-59)

Heaven is God's Presence & Hell is God's Absence

Most Christians in the nineteenth century believed the dead would be physically resurrected at the end of time. In a last judgment, Jesus would then separate "the sheep from the goats" (Matthew 25:32) and the eternally blessed would proceed, in their bodies, to heaven. This, of course, required a physical heaven. Hicks was rightly accused of denying the existence of this outward heaven.

To Hicks, this was backsliding to old covenant ways of thinking. That outward, physical covenant was expressed in outward, physical rites and rituals in this world and by an outward, physical heaven for the next world. But the new covenant initiated by Christ is inward and spiritual. Those who live under it know God as a spiritual being who exists in a boundless spiritual realm. Hicks looked to chapter fifteen in First Corinthians for a description of what happened when people die - they cast off their old, natural bodies and are clothed in new, spiritual ones. These spiritual bodies have no need for a physical heaven and would be immune to the torments of a physical hell.

"As to heaven and hell... Does not heaven signify a joyful state to the soul? And hell, a state of torment? And does not the presence of God, by his Spirit either justifying or condemning us, always produce those two states according to our obedience or disobedience to the divine requiring?... I consider that the torment of a soul separated from God by sin and transgression far exceeds what Jesus made use of as a figure thereof under the similitude of a body cast into a lake of fire and brimstone. But we cannot suppose that external fire and brimstone can have any effect on an immortal spirit." (Letters, pp. 257-58)

Hicks denied heaven is a physical place. To his opponents, this denied heaven was a real place and was further proof of his heresy.

Jesus' Role in Salvation

As discussed in the chapter on Jesus, the Epistle to the Hebrews states Jesus died for sins against the Law of the old covenant. As an outward event, Hicks believed the crucifixion was a shadow prefiguring the inward salvation Christians could experience under the gospel. Hicks summarized his views in a letter to William B. Irish in 1820. This argument was built on chapter nine in Hebrews and chapters six to eight in Romans.

> *"I consider that the offering of the body of Jesus Christ on the outward cross applied only, as a matter of redemption, to the Israelites – redeeming them from the curse of that covenant and the penalties attendant on any breach thereof. And this outward redemption was the top-stone of that figurative dispensation, as by it, that dispensation with all its legal rites and ceremonies was abolished and done away. Hence the Jews could no longer be guilty of any of those legal crimes, as the law that required those legal rites was dead and done away by the outward death of their Messiah. And this outward redemption of the outward bodies of the Israelites from the curses of their outward law and covenant is a complete figure of the inward redemption of the soul from sin by the life or spiritual blood of Christ inwardly sprinkling our consciences – and thereby enabling us to die to sin as he died for sin, by which we are redeemed from dead works to serve the living God in newness of life, which makes the true Christian." (Letters, p. 78)*

Atonement

To most Christians, Jesus died for the sins of all. The crucifixion was an act of atonement that reconciled humanity with God and opened a way to salvation.

There are various explanations of atonement; none has been formally adopted as the correct formulation of the doctrine. One theory of atonement states that humanity was in bondage to sin and, by his death, Jesus paid a ransom, thereby releasing all from spiritual imprisonment. Another version declares human sins insult God's honor and Jesus' death placated God's righteous anger. However atonement is supposed to work, the assumption is that the crucifixion was essential for human salvation.

Hicks would have none of it. The God he knew experientially, who had entered into the new covenant with humanity, did not require or desire human sacrifice and would certainly never have created anyone for the sole purpose of having that person horribly executed. In a closely reasoned letter to Phebe Willis, he drew on both scripture and reason to reject any theory of atonement that claimed spiritual merit for an outward act. Only sincere repentance, total submission to the directives of the Inward Light, and an inward, spiritual transformation of the heart and soul can atone for a person's sins and heal his or her relationship with the divine.

> *"To suppose, in this day of advanced Light, that the offering of the outward body of Jesus Christ should purge away spiritual corruption is entirely inconsistent with the nature and reason of things – as flesh and spirit bear no analogy with each other. And it likewise contradicts our Lord's own doctrines, where he assured the people that the flesh profiteth nothing... And I believe, nothing ever did or ever will atone for spiritual corruption, but the entire death of that from whence that corruption originated, which is the corrupt will and the life that the creature has generated in him by that will... And this is the true atonement, which the creature cannot effect for himself – only as he submits to the operation of the Life and Spirit of Christ, which will enable the willing and obedient to do it. And the outward atonement was a figure of it, which – with the outward example of Jesus Christ in his righteous works and pious death – gives strength to be faithful to make this necessary offering and sacrifice unto [God], by which his sins are blotted, and he again reconciled to his Maker."* (Letters, p. 98)

Christ died outwardly, pointing the way for each person to inwardly die to sin.

Rejected Notions about Salvation

Original Sin

Hicks believed every child is born innocent - Adam's and Eve's descendants have not inherited a stain of original sin on their souls that needs to be washed away. The same innate justice that motivates God to provide each person with the sure guidance of the Inward Light of Christ also ensures each has a pure and spotless start in life.

> *"As to original sin – according to the acceptance of some professors of Christianity, that we are under the curse for the transgression of our first parents – I abhor the idea as it casts a great indignity on the divine character to think that a gracious and merciful God should condemn us for an act that was wholly out of our power to avoid. I consider it very little short (if any) of blasphemy against God."* (Letters, p. 227)

Works Righteousness

Many Protestants subscribe to the belief that salvation is by grace alone and deny the possibility people can earn salvation by their own acts. Nothing anyone does, they assert, is sufficient to require God to grant salvation. It might seem that when Hicks called for righteous actions, he was advocating salvation by "works righteousness."

Hicks rejected salvation by works on two closely related grounds. First, individuals are capable of doing good only because they are enabled to do so by the grace of God. Second, there is no spiritual merit for actions people decide to do on their own. That comes only when they do those things to which the Light Within has pointed them.

Rising during worship in his home meeting in September 1815, he felt inspired to speak:

"My mind was quickened in the remembrance of the following declaration of the apostle Paul, 'By grace are ye saved through faith, and that not of yourselves. It is the gift of God, not of works, lest any man should boast.'

"The subject opened to communication, wherein I had to unfold to the people the utter incapacity man lay under (in his fallen or natural state) of doing anything that would in the least degree further his salvation or be acceptable to God... indeed, it would be justifiable to boast if we could do the least thing of ourselves without the immediate aid of divine grace. For strict justice cannot deny the ascription of merit to any cause that produces a real good work. But as no mere man can possibly ever be such a cause, so he can never merit any good from his own works, and therefore, never have a right to boast. All this, the truly humble are abundantly sensible of, and therefore dare not attempt anything in a religious way in their own time and will but wait patiently for the immediate inspiring of divine grace – to whose power only, as the procuring cause of our salvation, all merit is due." (Journal, pp. 240-241)

Faithfulness to God's will, however, requires action. A mere, passive faith is insufficient for salvation. God created the universe and placed humanity in it with the expectation that they would do the good works to which they were directed by the Light of Christ.

In 1815, Hicks held a public meeting in Newtown Kills, New York. At the close of the meeting, a Presbyterian minister engaged him in debate. Among other things, Hicks said:

"Faith in the sufficiency of the grace is the first previous work of the mind of man. But if that belief is not carried into effect, that faith cannot save him –

for faith without works is dead, being alone, just as the body without the spirit." (Journal, p. 220)

Hicks realized that undertaking good works - even work that is undeniably good in and of itself - can be spiritually destructive, because Satan wants nothing more than for people to follow their hearts and their own desires rather than the guidance of the Light Within - in other words, to believe they have the right to determine what is good and what they ought to be doing. When people succumb to this temptation, they set their own wills and their own desires above God's. Early Friends called this "will-worship." This transforms any good works they accomplish into false idols and the work into idolatry.

"I was led to show to the people how the mystery of iniquity [Satan] had wrought in and under every dispensation of God to the Church through his varied transformations - always resembling as much as may be, an angel of light - by which he lies in wait to deceive, and has generally deceived, and still deceives, the greater part of the people of all the nations under heaven - setting up his post by God's post, and leading his votaries to perform their worship and works just like the Lord's servants, with only this difference - that it's done in a way and time of their own heart's devising. And there is no other distinguishing mark than that the Lord's children are all taught of the Lord. And they are made to know it, for in righteousness they are established, and great is the peace of these children. But there is no peace to the wicked - to such as walk in their own wills and in the way of their own heart's devising." (Journal, pp. 295-96)

Earlier in his journal, Hicks had elaborated on this theme, bluntly describing work people choose for themselves as "evil." On the other hand, a faithful act - no matter how lowly or insignificant it might seem to be - is of incalculable spiritual value:

"But the great error of the generality of professed Christians lies in not making a right distinction between the works that men do in their own will and by the leadings of their own carnal wisdom, and those works that the true believer does in the will and wisdom of God. For although the former - let them consist in what they will, whether in prayers, or preaching, or any other devotional exercises - are altogether evil. So on the contrary, those of the latter - let them consist in what they may, whether in plowing, in reaping, or in any handicraft labor, or in any other service, temporal or spiritual, as they will in all be accompanied with the peace and presiding of

their Heavenly Father – so all they do will be righteous and will be imputed to them as such." (Journal, p. 220)

Imputed Righteousness

According to some theologians, humanity can only be reconciled with God by the imputation of Christ's righteousness. People, in other words, are depraved sinners and cannot ever justify themselves, but the righteousness of Jesus can be attributed to them. When that happens, they are treated as if they are righteous – even though they are not. This imputed righteousness is a gift granted purely by the grace of God and secured by faith alone.

Hicks condemned this view of salvation as requiring God to lie – to say a wicked person is virtuous – and for God to act as if that lie is the truth. But a person is either righteous or sinful, just or unjust, and it would violate the divine nature to pretend otherwise. Hicks believed that faith, without faithfulness, cannot reconcile anyone with God. This was also addressed in his Newtown Kills debate.

"Now will any be so inconsistent with Truth and Righteousness as to assert that a man is justified merely by the imputative righteousness that Christ wrought in the outward manifestation – without his coming to know in his own experience, those works of righteousness wrought in him... And which he must be a party in or they cannot be wrought, as mere grace (or a mere belief in grace) does not do the work of righteousness." (Journal, pp. 219-20)

Salvation and justification, Hicks asserted, were only available to those who were in fact righteous and the only way to live a righteous life was by complete submission to the leadings of the Inward Light.

"As I was sitting in our meeting, my mind became exercised in contemplating on the danger that some of my fellow professors of the Christian name are exposed to by placing their chief dependence for justification and salvation on the imputative righteousness of Christ performed without them – without coming to know a complete remission of their sins, and living a life of righteousness through faith in the operation of God, and a submission to the work of his Spirit in their minds – by which (according to the apostle's exhortation) they can only be enabled to work out their own salvation with fear and trembling, as it is God that worketh in the willing and obedient soul – both to will and to do of his own good pleasure. But this can only be witnessed by such as experience their

own wills to be mortified and slain by the power of the cross inwardly revealed, whereby the true spiritual atonement is made and the man of sin in us sacrificed." (Journal, p. 175)

Moreover, anyone who would accept salvation by imputed righteousness clearly did not deserve to receive it.

"Surely, is it possible that any rational being, that has any right sense of justice or mercy, would be willing to accept forgiveness of his sins on such terms? Would he not rather go forward and offer himself wholly up to suffer all the penalties due to his crimes, rather than the innocent should suffer? Nay! Was he so hardy as to acknowledge a willingness to be saved through such a medium, would it not prove he stood in direct opposition to every principle of justice and honesty, of mercy and love, and show himself to be a poor, selfish creature, unworthy of notice?" (Letters, p. 173)

True Christianity

"For true Christianity is nothing else but a real and complete mortification of our own will, and a full and final annihilation of all self-exaltation." *(Journal, p. 110)*

In the seventeenth century, the Religious Society of Friends declared it had revived Christianity as it had originated with Jesus and his first disciples. Primitive Christianity, they said, had been lost when the church lost its way and fell into apostasy. The church of the apostles had been partially recovered by earlier Protestant reformers, but they had completed the job. The lives of those who claimed to be the true successors of the first century disciples were built on waiting patiently for the immediate direction of the Holy Spirit - quieting their own wills, so they could hear and faithfully follow the guidance of the Light Within.

Elias Hicks accepted this account unequivocally. Late in his life, he exchanged letters with Joseph Plummer in which Hicks called on Friends in Indiana to remember that foundation - to stand still and quiet, trusting in God to guide them - in the face of the provocation they endured following the division of their yearly meeting.

> *"Friends are settled and established on the everlasting foundation - the Light Within or Spirit of Truth, by which God and his will are revealed to his rational creation, and upon which Jesus declared to his disciples he would build his church, against which the gates of hell should never be able to prevail. [Friends] ought not to be shaken or disturbed in mind, but stand still in the Lord, and he will bring about the overthrow of all that rise up against him and who do not believe in the sufficiency of his Light and grace for their salvation."* (Letters, p. 252)

Complete & Passive Obedience

A Quaker life is one of submission and discipline. When listing "the three principal requisites to the being and well-being of a Christian," Hicks listed first "a real belief in God and Christ," and "secondly, a complete, passive obedience and submission to the divine will and power - inwardly and spiritually manifested - which when known, brings to the Christian state through a crucifixion of the old man with all his ungodly deeds." (*Journal*, p. 349)

Absolute submission produced spiritual regeneration. This might result in an individual taking on the title of Christian - or Quaker - but formal membership was not essential. As Hicks noted in his journal:

"Therefore, no man or woman is any further Christians than as they come to experience the self-denial, meekness, humility and gentleness of Christ as the lamb of God who taketh away the sin of the world, ruling and reigning in them, so as to become their real life - in and by which, they become partakers of the divine nature and know the life of God raised up in the immortal soul. This is the new birth, or Christ formed in us, and without which, as our Lord told Nicodemus, no man can see the kingdom of God." (Journal, p. 110)

After wasting his adolescent years, Hicks had experienced such a "crucifixion of the old man" and a "new birth" spiritually as a new man. In this new life, he knew nothing was too trivial to be a divine concern. Any time people thought they could decide anything for themselves, they had wandered off the path of true Christianity:

"When the creature, in his own will, takes the liberty of judging for himself of what is little or what is great, he departs from the true standard and has no certain evidence to walk by. For if he has a right to judge for himself in one case, why not in every other? Here, doubting will arise in his mind of what is or is not agreeable to the Divine Will, as nothing can give the mind certain evidence, but faithfully complying with the evident sensations which the Light of Truth opens upon it - let them be what the creature may judge to be small or great. For we have no more reason or right to refuse complying with a small requisition than we have a great one, if the requisition proceeds from the same cause." (Journal, p. 378)

There is a danger intrinsic in any religion based on each individual's personal experience of the Spirit. It can leave each adherent isolated and vulnerable to the belief that he or she can determine what is right and true. To counteract this inclination, Friends have traditionally tested their leadings against the discernment of their local congregations. This requires meeting together, the third of "the three principal requisites."

"And thirdly, in order for the preservation and well-being of a Christian, it is necessary that they often meet and assemble together for the promotion

of love and good works, and as good stewards of the manifold grace of God – for which purpose, the Lord's people and children in all ages have been led by his Spirit to appoint times and seasons in which to present themselves before him." (Journal, p. 349)

Outward Rites & Rituals

Hebrews 9:10 speaks of "meats and drinks, and divers washings, and carnal ordinances, imposed on them until the time of reformation." Based in part on this verse, the earliest Friends had declared the need for any physical rites or rituals was over – the "time of reformation" had come. Following in their footsteps, Hicks rejected all outward rites and rituals as remnants of the old covenant that Jesus came into the world to fulfill and end:

"Jesus Christ in his outward body on the tree ... abolished the law of carnal commandments... Therefore, as there is no law now requiring those meats and drinks, and divers washing baptisms, and carnal ordinances... there can be no sin in the omission of all these under the gospel dispensation, as the law that made them binding is done away and abolished. Of the like nature also was their Seventh-Day Sabbath and all their other legally instituted holy days, as the law that enforced them is at an end." (Journal, pp. 175-76)

For Friends, baptism is a purely spiritual transformation that takes place within the soul – physical water cannot generate this inward change. Nor is there any spiritual benefit in eating bread or drinking wine. The only outward thing required is a faithful life. For Hicks, as for the earliest Quakers, "those who do not use them [outward rituals] may be effectually saved without them, if they attend to those things that are essential, *viz.*, justice, mercy, and faith." (*Letters*, p. 124)

True Ministers & True Ministry

In true Christianity, God selects, prepares, and ordains a person as a gospel minister. The only preparation for ministry an individual can pursue is to live a life of moral and spiritual development. In a letter to William Poole, Hicks declared:

"I cannot conceive that any can arrive to a state fit for gospel ministry until they have first fulfilled the substance of the moral law as Jesus did. And that opens the way for the reception of a further infusion of the Holy Spirit as a necessary preparation for gospel ministry. For every one who

ministers of the things of God must first be born of the Spirit of God – for none can be the sons of God, but those who are born of his Spirit." (Letters, p. 168)

Of Women Keeping Silence in the Churches

Service in the ministry is not restricted to those who attend a seminary or some other human institution. No single person or learned faculty could choose or prepare anyone. More importantly, no one can be excluded whom God has included. Even in the seventeenth century, the Religious Society of Friends recognized that both women and men are divinely chosen. In an 1820 letter, Hicks condemned the presumption of mere humans who think they could know who was or was not a minister:

"Consider the bold intrusions of the clergy on the divine prerogative – whose exclusive right it is to prepare, instruct, qualify and ordain both men and women to preach the gospel... and who, by their unhallowed human authority, have wholly excluded the female sex from any part therein, although divers of them nobly filled that important trust in the primitive churches." (Letters, p. 93)

Quaker acceptance of women speaking during worship - even young girls, servants, and women who were not formally recognized as ministers - had been controversial from the earliest days of the religious society. Starting with George Fox, Quaker leaders have been more than willing to enter the fray in their defense. When a correspondent cited what was viewed as a prohibition in First Corinthians, Hicks replied with an uncompromising scriptural defense:

"Of women keeping silence in the churches... Paul assures us that male and female are both one in Christ – that is, when they become real Christians, of whom Christ is the head. Also, under the law, there were prophetesses as well as prophets, and the diffusion of the Spirit in the latter day, as prophesized by Joel, was to be equally on sons and daughters, servants and handmaidens. And to believe otherwise is irrational and inconsistent with the divine attributes, and would impeach the Almighty with partiality and injustice to one-half of his rational creation." (Letters, pp. 82-83)

Hicks believed absolute equality was the fruit of utter submission to the divine will.

Worship in Spirit and in Truth

After being appointed by God, a minister should preach only those words chosen and qualified by divine inspiration. The idea that anyone would or should compose a sermon ahead of time was completely contrary to Quaker faith and practice. In a traditional meeting for worship, all present - including recognized ministers - were expected to completely still their hearts, minds, and wills, so they could fully open themselves up to the immediate leadings of the Holy Spirit. Only then could they hope to receive and deliver the message God intended for that particular gathering at that particular moment. To Friends, this was the worship "in spirit and in truth" Jesus had promised in the fourth chapter of John's gospel.

Silent Worship

Elias Hicks recognized that Friends' traditional meeting for worship was difficult for those who were used to the forms of worship common in other denominations. In his travels, Hicks frequently held public meetings and, therefore, would have repeatedly found himself in such a situation, but he trusted in the Spirit of Truth to guide him and to prepare and instruct the congregation.

> *"This [meeting for worship] proved a pretty exercising season by reason of the rawness and ignorance of some who attended - especially in the silent part of the meeting - being brought up and educated in the belief and habit that without they are engaged in some bodily exercise, such as outward and vocal singing, praying, preaching, or the like, there is no meeting - being so instructed by their blind teachers that it is very difficult to get them into stillness or into any right condition to hear. This makes hard work for the true gospel minister, whose labor and travail is to get into, and bring others into, a state of true solemn silence, that he may thereby become baptized into the state of the people, and be thereby qualified to administer to their real conditions - for otherwise preaching is vain. But as I continued patient in travail, my mouth was opened in a large, searching testimony, showing the fallacy and emptiness of all outward, ceremonial worship, and how it must inevitably land all those who trust therein in a state of sad disappointment in the end."* (Journal, pp. 355-56)

The task of speaking to the spiritual conditions of a diverse assemblage must have been daunting and, sometimes, he reported he was unable to do any more than to "example them to silence." Even so, as a measure of his success in meeting the spiritual needs of his listeners, when he announced a public meeting, even the largest venues were frequently filled to overflowing.

Prepared Sermons

To nineteenth-century Friends, whenever people prepared a sermon or pre-planned worship, they put themselves in spiritual peril. This custom was neither expedient nor prudent, because, in so doing, the creature sought to become the Creator and risked being snared by Satan.

> *"And such is the working of the deceiving spirit in man that those who give way in man's ability and science to preach what they have culled out of their own brain or human abilities – it tends more and more to exalt them in a belief of their own sufficiency and lessens their dependence and trust in God, insomuch that they often desert him entirely and preach only from the letter. For take away their written notes and they are all dumb. And nothing is more necessary for a rightly inspired gospel minister than to keep a strict and continual watch over his own spirit – that it may not get up and mingle its own imaginary thoughts with the divine openings. For many have fallen that way for want of greater watchfulness in keeping self continually under the power of the cross until the old man with all his deeds are crucified." (Letters, p. 208)*

Formal Prayers

Even for a speaker to recite a prayer that was not inspired in the moment was spiritually dangerous. The words of a prepared prayer may have been spiritually significant when they were first spoken, but in repetition, they risked being "formal, lifeless communications." In fact, to use such a prayer was "an abomination in the sight of the Lord." True prayer passed through the person praying like breath passes through a flute – as a human instrument passively played by a divine performer.

In one of the few letters he sent to a woman outside of his family, Hicks reflected on how to pray:

> *"For I consider it to require our minds being clothed with deep reverence and Godly fear to approach and address the Majesty of Heaven in solemn prayer… the Lord, I believe, in the present day as formerly, sees meet in his wisdom and goodness to inspire the hearts of his ministers… with the spirit of prayer and supplication. Not to inform him of their wants – which he altogether knows – but as a means to prepare the minds of such disconsolate ones with faith and courage suitably to look up to him as their*

only helper – which places them in a condition to receive his blessing with gratitude and thanksgiving." (Letters, pp. 190-91)

Singing

Nevertheless, an individual may be divinely led to recite a beloved prayer because it accurately reflected that person's spiritual condition in the moment. Even more so, a single person might be inspired to sing a psalm or a hymn that gave voice to the true condition of his or her soul. But Hicks could not conceive of a circumstance when the hearts of each and every member of a congregation were truly revealed in the words of a song sung by all.

"I have long been convinced of the impropriety of vocal singing in Christian congregations... or of using any forms of prayer of man's making, and of all set times to pray, to sing, or preach... the Christian man cannot... premeditate or indite beforehand any form of prayer by which to address the Majesty of Heaven – or invent any psalm or hymn by which to give praise to him – without an infringement of the divine prerogative, but must wait in humble submission in the silence of all flesh and all fleshly desires, until he feels his mind immediately inspired by the Spirit of Truth, inwardly dictating to the mind what it shall say, or how it shall (consistent with the divine will) perform those sacred duties of prayer and praise – whether by vocal voice or in secret, silent aspirations – begotten in the passive obedient soul immediately by the Spirit of God." (Letters, pp. 204-205)

Challenges

If he were to visit with Quakers today, Elias Hicks would certainly be amazed any congregation of Friends would presume to call an individual to be their minister or pastor, much less to decide ahead of time on songs to sing, prayers to pray, and scriptures to read in worship. He might well dismiss them as not being true Quakers – perhaps noting sadly that this was the inevitable end to which the Orthodox were headed.

Unprogrammed Friends might confidently suggest he come worship with them, only to be surprised by his reaction to all the programming he would encounter there – hymn-singing before meeting for worship (and sometimes during worship), queries read during worship, or an invitation for "joys and concerns" to be shared. There are very few meetings that come together in silence and worship God in the manner of Friends he would have experienced two hundred years ago.

Of course, Hicks would also be dismayed to see people show up for meeting in sandals, shorts, and a Hawaiian shirt; and would be horrified when the greeter reached to shake his hand and cheerfully exclaimed, "Welcome, Mr. Hicks!"

Much has changed in the nearly two centuries since the last time Hicks embarked on a religious visit among Friends and others, but I believe Hicks (after recovering from momentary shock) would recognize the outward rites and rituals of twenty-first-century Friends - both pastored and unprogrammed - are expendable. They are the outer wrappings, not the inner essence, of what it means to be a Friend.

His challenge would not be to see if we can dress or talk like nineteenth-century Friends, but if we can be utterly faithful to the leadings of the Inward Light. The wider society we live in celebrates personal freedom and cherishes the individual's right to choose what to do and how to do it. This is diametrically opposed to "a complete, passive obedience and submission to the divine will and power."

Do we have the patience to wait for our leadings to be clear?

Do we have the strength and humility to follow wherever we are led?

Applied Quakerism

"I consider God only to be the real author of all true faith. I have always endeavored to keep it clear of all tradition and education, and that it always might stand on the unshaken foundation – the alone revelation of the Father." (Letters, p. 158)

Truth-telling & Tolerance

One of the most characteristic attributes of the early Religious Society of Friends was its embrace of radical truth-telling. This had wide-ranging consequences on the lives of its members; resulting in such practices as setting a fixed price when selling goods and refusing to swear an oath, even in court. These are fondly remembered and celebrated by Quakers today.

The same standards also caused difficulties in personal relationships. Radical truth-telling led Quakers to reject the use of those simple pleasantries that lubricate social interactions – removing, or at least tipping, one's hat ("hat honor") or greeting a friend with "Good day, kind sir." This gained them a reputation for being brusque and even rude. Over time, these expectations eroded. It was difficult to go through life without using "the common greetings of the day" or telling the little white lies that are nearly second nature for people who think of themselves as kind and considerate.

Being members of a minority religious sect with very different doctrines from the religious mainstream, raised another question: how to avoid telling the neighbors they are wrong about things of ultimate spiritual importance? For Hicks, the answer was simple. Tell the truth, even if it hurts feelings and might cost friendships – a position some Quakers found harsh:

"[Some Friends] are ready to criminate their brethren for publicly opposing and exposing those false doctrines, and such like opinions and tenets of others – although they themselves believe them to be false. But they love to

keep up a fair side to all, least as they say, they will give offence – and so balk their testimony rather than lose the friendship and (what is still more with them I fear) the praise of men." (Letters, pp. 89-90)

Disagreement & Friendship

This might give the impression Hicks was intolerant of others' opinions, but this was far from the case. While he objected to Friends speaking less than the truth, Hicks considered tolerance of others' religious beliefs to be a central tenant of Quakerism. Indeed, when the Great Separations took place in 1827-28, he didn't refer to his allies as Hicksites, but as the "Tolerants." Even so, being tolerant of other people doesn't mean hiding one's own convictions.

In 1825-26, he exchanged a few letters with Barnabas Bates, the editor of a magazine titled *The Christian Inquirer*. Bates was not a Friend. He had served as a Baptist preacher before joining the Unitarians. With one of his letters, Bates enclosed a gift for Hicks from a mutual friend – a book of hymns. Hicks' reply was cordial, while at the same time, it clearly expressed his views on how God should be worshipped. In particular, he singled out singing as inappropriate in religious services:

"I have no unity with any psalms or hymns indited and prepared by man for any religious purpose – considering them all below the dignity of gospel dispensation, as all its religion and worship is purely spiritual…

"And although I highly esteem the kindness of thy friend in presenting me with the volume alluded to – and which I consider on his part an act of sincere friendship and for which I return him my hearty thanks, even as though it had been one fully to my liking – yet, as I apprehend it would be to me a loss of time to read it, it appears best for me to return it, and which may give him an opportunity to present it to some other that approves of singing in worship and be edified with its contents.

"Hoping that our different views on such subjects, while we cherish in each other the tolerant spirit of the gospel, will have no tendency to break or interrupt our friendship. In the fresh feeling of which, I subscribe thine and thy kind friend's sincere and affectionate well-wisher." (Letters, p. 207)

There were limits, however, to Hicks' tolerance. In his public ministry, he delighted in denouncing some of the doctrines of other Christians. In 1793, he held a public meeting at the courthouse in Portland, Maine in which "many doctrines of the gospel being clearly opened and the absurd doctrines of original sin, predestination, as also the schemes of the universalists, atheists, and deists [were] confuted from scripture and reason" (*Journal*, p. 54). Age did not mellow him. Thirty-five years later, a letter again decries "the incorrectness and absurdity of the doctrine of unconditional and personal election" (*Letters*, p. 227).

Nevertheless, non-Quakers had an absolute right to believe whatever nonsense they desired!

The Plain Speech

Another aspect of Quaker adherence to truth-telling was the use of "thee," "thou," "thy," and "thine" when speaking to a single individual. Even in the nineteenth century, this was an archaic form in English. In earlier times, these pronouns had been used when speaking with a social peer or an inferior. Correspondingly, as a sign of respect, a person from a higher social class had every right to expect to be addressed with the plural forms, "you," "your," and "yours." (Curiously, God was denied this token of respect.)

Early Friends insisted that using the singular forms for a single person was merely recognizing an obvious truth. More importantly, it avoided flattery. By the late eighteenth century, the English language had evolved in a very different direction, with everyone being accorded the formal, polite plural pronouns. Quakers maintained their practice, even though the reasons for it had been completely undercut.

In his use of "the plain speech," Elias Hicks was an unstinting traditionalist, but he justified the custom with a unique defense. First, he declared the Quaker practice to be more important than the outward ordinances - a contention that may have been accepted by Friends of the time - but his second defense may reveal his lack of formal education. Making a scriptural argument, he appears to contend that Jesus and the prophets actually spoke the form of English found in the King James Version of the Bible:

> *"The plain grammatical language of 'thee' and 'thou' to a single person - being the only correct and plain language of Truth and of the Scriptures - I deem much more essential than water baptism or the partaking of bread and wine in a ceremonial way as a religious act... the Scriptures throughout (which being the language of all the holy men of old and only language of plain truth) have made use of it of all times - which I consider an unequivocal testimony of its essentiality - because it is contrary to the*

reason and nature of things to suppose that they should have always thus kept to it had they not thought it essential." (Letters, pp. 123-24)

Interestingly, a generation after his death, most Friends abandoned plain speech, considering it to be an outward form without spiritual merit, although some continued to use it within their meetings and their families.

A Marriage of Equals

"I was led... to open the true ground of the marriage covenant – whereby male and female may be rightly joined together, so as to become true helpmeets and blessings to each other." (Journal, p. 323)

In addition to advocating a woman's right to preach the gospel, Hicks advocated full equality for Quaker women in their homes and in their marriages. This went well beyond the standards of nineteenth-century American society. It is instructive to notice, however, that his scriptural basis required both men and women to unconditionally submit to the authority of God in order for equality to be achieved. In a letter to William Poole, he wrote:

"When our first parents set up a will and turned away from that passive state that they ought ever to have stood in to the divine will, God graciously ordained that the woman should be subject to her husband, and he should rule over her, and this subjection ought to continue until both surrender their wills again to God as in the beginning. And the male and female will be one in him. And then man's sovereignty over the woman is entirely done away, and God's will becomes all in all." (Letters, p. 106)

This changes the nature of marriage – each is equally a helpmeet to the other, but for a couple to come into this favored relationship required a common understanding of one's commitment to God. This is one reason Friends took seriously Paul's admonition in 2 Corinthians 6:14, "Be ye not unequally yoked together with unbelievers." Quakers who married non-Quakers could face great difficulty in finding such mutuality of belief. Even so, marriages between members and non-members did take place. Apparently, at least some meetings were willing to allow the wedding if the non-member submitted to Quaker practice.

However, if the wedding was conducted by a priest or hireling minister, the couple was blatantly rejecting Quaker standards and the member would be labored with to "come to a sense of their error." A member unwilling to acknowledge the breach of good order would be disowned, but could be restored if they apologized to the meeting. In this case, the marriage was recognized by the meeting.

Hicks supported this practice unequivocally, but his concern went a step further. Too often, he felt, couples set themselves and their children on a path to unhappiness by marrying for the wrong reasons. This misfortune, he believed, could be unfailingly avoided if before marrying, members simply sought the guidance of the Inward Light in choosing a life partner:

> *"Scarcely one in ten thousand of the human family even think of seeking first the kingdom of God or its righteousness – or even asking counsel of him [God] in the weighty concern of marriage, upon a right procedure in which, their present and future happiness greatly depends. And for want of this right, previous care, families are mostly unhappy by their going forward in their own wills, and according to their own natural lusts and affections. They are often very unequally yoked together. And when these have a family of children about them without any right ability and qualification to instruct them, confusion and disorder ensued. And the poor children are left to grow up without right cultivation, as the bushes in the wilderness, a lamentable case indeed – a view of which has often clothed my mind with mourning on behalf of these." (Journal, p. 291)*

A Guarded Education

Protection of children from the harmful influences of the world needed to begin at birth. Moral and religious instruction began in the cradle, but children also needed to be able to read, write, and do their numbers. For many children, elementary education was all they would need and all they would receive. Schooling was important, but it had to be fit in around the many tasks children were assigned in their home and to help in the family's business. Whenever possible, Friends provided their children with a "guarded education" – that is, schooling taught by Quakers and in classes made up of other Quaker children.

To meet the needs of their children, most Friends Meetings supported a primary school; some also provided secondary education, often with a boarding school that was open to children from other meetings. Although in all likelihood, Elias Hicks received very little formal education, he gave his time generously to both of these endeavors. He was an occasional teacher in the Jericho Friends primary school and served on the governing board of Nine Partners School, a boarding secondary school in Millbrook,

New York (still surviving as Oakwood Friends School, now in Poughkeepsie, New York). He doesn't mention her, but he likely encountered Lucretia Mott during her years at Nine Partners, first as a student and later as an assistant teacher.

In the 1810s, concern was raised in New York Yearly Meeting about the education of Quaker youth. This may have been in reaction to the recent establishment of public schools. After due consideration, the subordinate quarterly meetings were instructed to appoint visiting committees "in order to further stir up Friends to this concern." Elias Hicks was chosen for one of these itinerant committees and commented on the committee's work in his journal:

> *"I have a hope that Friends will be strengthened and encouraged to persevere in the concern… for the religious and moral instruction of our youth while at school by placing them under the care of pious tutors, who may cooperate with the endeavors of religiously concerned parents, who are more desirous that their children may be brought up and educated in the fear of the Lord and in his nurture and admonition, than that they should make great advancements in scholastic science or in the riches and popularity of the world." (Journal, pp. 281-82)*

Right Reason

In a letter to his dear friend, William Poole, Hicks wrote, "None can believe what they do not understand" (*Letters,* p. 162). Because of statements like this, Hicks was accused of being a Deist and a Rationalist.

Rationalism, a product of Enlightenment philosophy, holds that knowledge is the product of reasoning. It is related to Deism, a belief that God created the universe, but does not intervene in it. This would include claiming divine revelation as a source of religious faith. Instead, Deism bases faith on human reason and observations of the natural world.

In his writings, William Penn frequently depended on a combination of scripture and "right reason" to support his positions. In the seventeenth century, when Penn was writing, the mind was understood to be a property of the soul, not a product of the brain, and "right reason" referred to reasoning under divine guidance, as opposed to ordinary rational thought.

Elias Hicks often cited arguments originally put forward by Penn, but Hicks may not have recognized the distinction between different qualities of reasoning. As a result, his re-statements of Penn's arguments may have seemed closer to rationalism than to traditional Quaker thought.

Hicks assumed God created humans as rational beings, equipping them with minds they could use to determine the truth of a proposition - even a religious one. Although he is not a rationalist - he is an advocate of continuing divine revelation - he believed ultimate Truth can be revealed by the God-given ability to reason.

> *"[People have] natural and civil rights to think and act for themselves... Hence arises the privilege of individual investigation and the equal right of withholding our assent to any proposition which we believe is not in accordance with truth and reason. And for any to attempt to enforce an assent to any position by mere power, without rational conviction, is arbitrary, oppressive, and tyrannical."* (Letters, p. 187)

Hicks rejected all claims of truth based solely on tradition or education, or on popular opinion and human customs. No one should believe what they do not understand.

Threats to Reason

There are, however, limits to what an individual can achieve by the power of reason. Some threats are external and easily identified. When, for example, people are subjected to overt pressure to conform, they naturally resist. More insidious are the threats that arise within the individual. Too many people (and here, he was probably thinking of those within the Society of Friends who disagreed with him) are not receptive of any argument that wasn't "congenial to self and selfish views," i.e., what they already believed:

> *"I have no doubt but Divine Wisdom and Impartial Goodness has opened a medium to every rational, intelligent mind, by which... every truth necessary to be known in the way of its salvation will be furnished. But if that is neglected and turned from... yet such will cavil and call for more clear evidence. As they disregard the evidence of Divine Truth in their own minds, so neither will they regard any other evidence."* (Letters p. 51)

Challenges

Much has changed since the founding of the Religious Society of Friends in the middle of the seventeenth century. In particular, radical truth-telling elicits few negative consequences - the world has accommodated and even co-opted Quaker practices in this respect. Most retail operations post fixed prices. The social distinctions upheld by "hat honor" and different second-person pronouns have faded almost to extinction and we have given up the corresponding testimonies. On the rare occasion a Friend is asked to swear an oath, there is always the option to "affirm."

But Friends have acclimated to the ways of the world at least as much as the world has adapted to us. Nearly all Quakers long ago abandoned wearing "the plain clothes" and speaking "the plain speech." Those few who continue to follow the old ways attract more curiosity than hostility - they are quaint, not threatening. We greet Quakers and non-Quakers alike with the "common greetings of the day" and are generally people who think of themselves as kind and considerate. Tolerance is as central to Friends identity as it has ever been. We extoll "speaking truth to power," but that rarely involves any risk.

So, does adherence to radical truth-telling ever make demands on our lives? Do we hold ourselves to a higher standard than what we expect from others? Is that ever difficult?

It may be more challenging to risk combining genuine disagreement with genuine friendship. Hicks was faced with making "Love your enemy" real in his life - and sometimes he failed in the attempt.

Do we "love to keep up a fair side to all, least... [we] give offence"?

Do we conceal our "testimony rather than lose the friendship"?

What do we risk for our faith?

The World

"I fear there is a considerable number under our name of this description, who not only love the world, but also its friendships, manners, maxims, policies, customs, fashions, vanities, pleasures, and amusements, yet like to bear the name of Quaker because it has become honorable among men. Alas! How much better would it be for the Society and the promotion of Truth if it was still a name of reproach among men!" (Letters p. 53)

At the time of Elias Hicks' birth, the Religious Society of Friends was in the process of a reformation. At the heart of this movement was the conviction that Quakers were becoming too swept up in the wider society of British North America. Between his birth in 1748 and the beginning of the American Revolution in 1775, the society was distilled to its essence. Disownments reduced the number of Friends and many of those disowned were young people, expelled for "marrying out." The province of Pennsylvania had been governed by a "Quaker Party" since its founding, but in 1762, Philadelphia Yearly Meeting advised its members to withdraw from all "offices or stations in civil government" and to abstain from voting or promoting others to run for office. Such activities were "inconsistent with our religious principles" and tended "to lay waste our Christian testimony." If members persisted, they were to be labored with and, "if they cannot see and acknowledge their error," they were to be disowned.[1]

At about this time, John Woolman gave up shop keeping and became a tailor. He felt he was becoming too successful at business and his success was drawing him too much into the world.[2] Tailoring afforded him a smaller income, but one that was adequate to the needs of his family.

---

[1] *The Old Discipline: Nineteenth-Century Friends' Disciplines in America*, Glenside, PA: Quaker Heritage Press, 1999, pp. 25-26.

[2] Moulton, Phillips P. (Ed.), *The Journal and Major Essays of John Woolman*. New York: Oxford University Press, 1971, p. 53.

Needless to say, Woolman was a wholehearted supporter of the Quaker reformation.

It was a generation of pulling back, purifying, and repairing the hedge that surrounded the religious society - separating and protecting it from the profane influences of the wider world. This was the environment of Elias Hicks' youth and young adulthood - the reform was in the air he breathed and the water he drank. It was how he expected things ought to be.

On Being a Peculiar People

During the American Revolution and in the years following, Quaker contact with "the world" increased, but Hicks' views did not change. He was over eighty years old when he collected his memoirs and included among them his recollection of ministry offered to a 1798 monthly meeting for business in Baltimore:

> *"I was led in a large, searching testimony to set forth the great danger and hurtful effects of Friends joining in with the spirit of the world, in taking any part in the fluctuating governments, customs, and manners thereof - things opening clearly to set forth how the apostasy took place through that medium, both among the primitive Christians and also in our own society in days past. And that the only way for us as a people to regain the primitive state was to return back into ancient simplicity by a separation from the world - its spirit, governments, manners, and maxims - and to make no league with those actuated thereby." (Journal, p. 73)*

Hicks had no doubt Friends are (or ought to be) a Light to the World - a critique, not a reflection of it. He trusted the Quaker example would build the kingdom of heaven on earth. At home in Jericho Meeting in 1818, he was moved to pray for Friends to fulfill their calling:

> *"And O, saith my soul! That we as a people, called as we are to be a light to the world, might so persevere in faithfulness and obedience to the teachings and inspiring of Light and Truth in our hearts. By which, we should be enabled to unite together for the exaltation of this noble testimony, and the increase of the spiritual Messiah's kingdom of truth, righteousness, and peace in the earth. And which, in its progression, will break down and dissolve all the kingdoms of this world, until they become the kingdoms of our Lord and of his Christ, and he comes to reign, whose right it is." (Journal, p. 337)*

The dangers of mixing with the people of the world were compounded when Friends were drawn into collective action in which their unique voices would be lost and the pressures to compromise their principles amplified. Hicks distrusted such corporate activities as the products of human, rather than divine, desires. The compromises that necessarily arose set an especially damaging example for younger members of the society. In 1819, Hicks ministered at the Pearl Street Meeting in New York City on this topic:

> *"My mind, soon after taking my seat, was brought under a renewed exercise on account of the members of our society mixing in with the associations of other people - in their governments and politics, their Bible and missionary societies, and pretended charity associations - which had a very hurtful tendency by leavening the minds of Friends, and leading them to assimilate with the spirit of the world, and turning them away from the simplicity of our profession... Such conduct is particularly wounding to some of the beloved youth... It leads them into a free familiarity and friendship with such as are light and vain in their conversation and deportment, by which their tender minds are greatly wounded, and they led off from the cross and a strict regard to that sobriety of conduct, which Truth requires of all its professors." (Journal, p. 376)*

Business & Commerce

Two hundred years ago, many Quakers deemed every waking hour as an opportunity to acknowledge the Holy Presence in their lives. Because most people spent the greatest part of their time making a living, business and commercial activities afforded the most frequent opportunities to put their religious beliefs to the test. John Woolman saw how success in operating a retail shop demanded more and more of his time and energy and interfered with his religious duties. His solution was to reduce his business dealings to the minimum necessary to pay the bills. This freed him for service and travel among Friends. Although not as stringent in reducing his duties, Elias Hicks undoubtedly commended the path John Woolman had followed.

Near the end of his life, Elias Hicks received a letter from Samuel Evans, a young man who was considering a career in the law. In reply, Hicks did not encourage the prospect. He distrusted lawyers and the use of courts to settle disputes - recommending mediation among neighbors as an alternative - but expressed at least as much concern for the time and attention a legal career would demand. His advice was to seek instead an occupation that left more room for God:

"There are a great variety of honest callings, in each of which every honest, industrious man can procure a sufficiency of this world's goods for his own and family's comfort – and which will much less interfere with our religious duty and conduce more to the general good of Society.

"I would recommend some mechanical branch, which will require but a small beginning, and which manner of life is generally conducive to health, and freer from care and less burdensome to the mind than some higher branches of business." (Letters, p. 264)

Elias Hicks also regularly corresponded with the painter Edward Hicks (a son of Elias' second cousin). In the late summer of 1822, Edward's workshop and tools were destroyed in a fire. In a letter, Elias offered condolences and noted he had also heard that Edward had taken seriously ill while traveling in the ministry. He then commented:

"Now, my dear Friend, are not these lessons of a very deep instruction? They show how very unfit and incapable we are of laying out or making any appointments of our own that will insure to us any real good – either in temporals or spirituals. And even when we proceed in his counsel... he does not leave it for us to judge how long or how far we may proceed therein, but he keeps the reins in his own hand." (Letters, p. 151).

In other words, man proposes; God disposes.

This led Elias to consider that many people – even some Friends – unconsciously slide from working to earn a sufficient income into an ultimately destructive grasping after unneeded riches:

"And many there are, I believe, who in their setting out in life may be rightly directed in their choice of business – by which to obtain a comfortable livelihood for themselves and families – and at which time, they neither thought of nor coveted more. But through the corrupt custom and course of trade and business among men in their fallen state, some increase their worldly possessions in such a rapid way – they soon obtain and amass together much more than they either desired or expected in their first setting out. And for want of keeping a single eye to their Divine Director, who, if rightly attended to, would as clearly have showed them where to stop as he showed them where to begin. But for want of this right attention, they have continued on. By which means, their desires after more have increased with the increase of their possessions – that finally they lose all right sense of what is right for them. And by grasping after

more in their own dark wisdom, they bring a blast on all their designs, and plunge themselves and families into irretrievable poverty and disgrace – while some others are permitted to proceed on until their minds are wholly swallowed up in their abundance, the care of which becomes such a load and burden that they have no rest. And it eventually terminates in the utter ruin of themselves and families as it respects their eternal condition. And their temporal abundance soon becomes squandered and lost by licentiousness and extravagance of their offspring or heirs – as such estates, thus gotten, seldom last longer than the second or third generation." (Letters, pp. 152-53)

Public Education

The guarantee of free public education is one of the great achievements of societies around the world. Where the schools are inadequate, governments are seen as failing to provide basic services. It may be a surprise to learn that Elias Hicks was not an advocate.

The public school movement grew rapidly in the early nineteenth century, with New York City playing a leading role. Prior to this time, many children went unschooled - perhaps learning in the home to sign their names or to read a little or to add and subtract, but too often, not even that. Children who received an education attended private schools or charity schools - for example, the school for girls established in New York in 1802 by the Association of Women Friends for the Relief of the Poor. Most schools were affiliated with one religious body or another.

On February 19, 1805, the first meeting of the New York Free School Society was held in the home of John Murray, Jr., a member of Flushing Meeting. Valentine Hicks, a son-in-law of Elias Hicks, may have been present and was, in any event, one of the leaders in establishing what grew into the New York public school system.

By today's standards, Hicks was a libertarian - governments should not interfere in things better done by individuals, families, or religious bodies. This would include staying out of primary education, since as discussed in the chapter, *Applied Quakerism*, Hicks held the education of children was one of the fundamental duties of parents.

In 1820, Hicks received a letter from Sylvanus Smith, who seems to have been involved in promoting public schools. (Smith may have been the father of Sarah Tomkins Garnet, the first African-American woman to serve as the principal of a New York City Public School.) Smith's letter was apparently a request that Hicks assist the movement in some way. The response was vehemently negative:

"I have been, ever since I have had children to educate, conscientiously restrained from sending them to any schools to be educated, except such as were under the immediate care of the Society of which I am a member... believing from the observations I have made, that my children would receive more harm by attending schools taught by persons of no religious principles and among children whose parents were of different sects (and many very loose and unconcerned and vulgar in their lives and conduct), than all the learning and science they could obtain at such schools could ever atone for. Hence, I considered it better and more consistent with my duty as a parent to keep my children at home... than to send them to such schools where the bad example and vicious conduct of many of the children (and sometimes even the teachers) would be very degrading to their morals and wounding to their tender minds... As the bringing up and right education of our children is a religious duty, and for which we are accountable to none but God only, therefore for the magistrate to interfere therewith by coercive means is an infringement upon the divine prerogative." (Letters, pp. 84-85)

In the same letter, Hicks offered an extended commentary on the taxes levied to support the new public schools in New York State. He considered these taxes unfair and an infringement on religious rights comparable to the "Blue Laws" that forbade commercial activity on Sundays. Friends, he declared, would never enroll their children in public schools, so they shouldn't have to pay for them.

An argument frequently made in favor of public schools is that they educate the children of people who could not afford private schools. Hicks supported this goal - just not to the way in which it was accomplished.

In addition to his service in the Jericho Meeting School and to the Nine Partners School, Hicks was a decades-long member of the governing committee of the Charity Society of Jericho and Westbury Monthly Meetings. This society was formed in 1794 "for the use and benefit of the poor among the Black people and more especially for the education of their children" (*Journal*, p. 165). It must be acknowledged, however, that this society did not enroll disadvantaged children in Quaker schools. In keeping with the prejudices of the day, the society funded separate schooling.

The Separation of Church & State

In October 1825, the Erie Canal was completed, linking Buffalo, New York on Lake Erie to Albany, New York on the Hudson River. This allowed barge traffic from the upper Great Lakes to move directly to the Atlantic Ocean without having to off-load at Niagara Falls. It enormously reduced the cost of shipping and gave the state a huge economic boost. This achievement was celebrated by a thanksgiving day proclaimed by the Governor of New York.

This was not Thanksgiving Day as celebrated today. Days of thanks were periodically proclaimed by the government to give God thanks for some great event (often a military victory). Less frequent were days of fasting for public repentance and reflection when things went badly. Quakers had historically refused to participate in any such days, considering them to be government-enforced religious events.

News of the governor's declaration was printed in *The Christian Inquirer*, a periodical Elias Hicks evidently had read, even though it was written for a general readership and edited by a Unitarian. In reaction, he was moved to write to Barnabas Bates, the editor.

The letter is remarkable in several ways. First, to modern Friends, the idea Quakers should not observe a thanksgiving may seem incredible - they may not consider it a religious celebration. For the same reason, Friends today might not view such a proclamation as breaching the separation of church and state, but Hicks saw that as the crux of the problem. Finally, it is notable Hicks cited, as part of his argument, the sacrifices made by soldiers in the American Revolution. In doing so, he displayed a (somewhat surprising) willingness to tailor his presentation to his audience - they valued military sacrifices. As such, it may give some insight into the content of his ministry in public meetings.

> *"Thanksgiving day... certainly comprehends a considerable breach on the wise and excellent constitution of these United States, and is, in effect, a surrendering up to clerical influence a considerable part of that freedom and liberty of conscience that our predecessors of '76 sacrificed their lives and their all for the purchase of...*
>
> *"Has not our chief magistrate... by recommending a religious act, united the civil and ecclesiastical authorities and broken the line of partition between them, so wisely established by our enlightened constitution - which in the most positive terms forbids any alliance between church and state, and is the only barrier for the support of our liberty and*

independence. For if that is broken down, all is lost and we become the vassals of priest-craft and designing men, who are reaching after power by every subtle contrivance to domineer over the consciences of their fellow citizens." (Letters, pp. 198, 200)

Public Life

"No man can serve two masters." (Matthew 6:24)

The fundamental reason Friends were advised to withdraw from all government service was it led to divided loyalties. The demands of the state and the obligations of membership in the Religious Society of Friends were seen as too often incompatible. Hicks saw this as an irresoluble dilemma even for the government established in Pennsylvania by William Penn. In an 1809 letter to John Murray, Jr., he was unequivocal in his rejection of any Quaker involvement:

"I very much doubt – although I esteem William Penn very highly for his noble surrender in his young days to the cross and his religious writings as very instructive and excellent – whether all his good works and excellent writings will be sufficient to atone for the hurt he has done Society by taking the province of Pennsylvania as a reward for his father's services in the wars of England and accepting the commission of governor from the king – by which he was considered as invested as an officer and servant of an earthly prince at the same time as he was professing to be a servant and minister of Jesus Christ... that is, to be heirs of two kingdoms and to endeavor to serve two masters." (Letters, pp. 19-20)

Governments are by Nature Violent

A second reason for concern about Quaker participation in government was the ultimate foundation of civil authority. If pressed hard enough, every government will resort to coercion and violence to preserve itself. At Jericho Meeting in 1815, during the War of 1812, Hicks offered ministry on the essential nature of human governments:

"[I] was led to contrast those who are led and influenced by the wisdom and will of man, with those who are led and influenced by the wisdom and will of God, and was let to see how of necessity the former must be ruled and governed by the wisdom and power of man – hence the necessity of coercion, and hence the necessity of war, as every government of coercion must of necessity be set up and maintained by the force and fear of the

sword or other armor efficient to take life, as that is the last alternative in every government set up in the wisdom and will of man." (Journal, p. 208)

Politics

One seemingly inevitable consequence of holding elections is the appearance of political parties. Many people do not themselves hold political offices, but participate in the political process by actively supporting one party or another. They believe it is a way to fulfill their responsibility to play a part in a self-governing society. Those who feel they cannot serve in government might, at least, work to ensure that those who did were the best people available.

In the 1760s, the Society of Friends regarded even this as leading to unacceptable entanglement in political disputes and the discord they engendered. In his letter to John Murray, Hicks expanded on this, pointing out political parties have their own objectives and will manipulate their supporters to achieve their goals.

"There is no one thing that causes so much breach of unity and want of harmony among Friends there [in Pennsylvania], as the part they take in promoting what they call civil government – some joining with one part and some with the other. And I believe there is nothing else that reproaches so much in the eyes of the people without [outside the Society of Friends], although each party endeavors to persuade them to it – although only to make tools of them, to promote their party interests." (Letters, p. 21)

Don't Vote

What the religious society called for was complete withdrawal from all participation, at any level and to any degree. Don't hold office. Don't support a party. Don't advocate for a candidate. And finally, don't vote. Only in this way can Friends stand clear of being ensnared in the coercion and violence inherent in politics and governing.

His letter to John Murray celebrated evidence that younger Friends were following these standards:

"I observed one thing when traveling in Pennsylvania that afforded much satisfaction and encouragement. Many of the younger and middle-aged class appeared to be inspired with a true zeal and concern on those accounts, and were fast withdrawing from taking any active part in the government or even voting at their elections – although much urged thereto (as they informed me) by some of their old, warm, party brethren. I

had conversation with many of them and I was glad in finding they had some of the most experienced elders in that country as their encouragers." (Letters, p. 20)

War

War is Blasphemy

Friends were unambiguous in their corporate opposition to all war and all participation in wars. Not only is killing wrong and the destruction of war horrendous (even in the early nineteenth century); war is a sacrilege – a denial of God. As Hicks stated in a letter to a man reconsidering his career in government:

"And are not the armies of Christendom guilty of all kinds of blasphemy? For do they not in word and conduct blaspheme both God and man… shedding the blood of saints and martyrs, and the millions slain in the wars – the cruel wars – of Christendom." (Letters, pp. 92-93)

Praying for Victory is an Abomination

With such an understanding, prayers for victory are not merely misguided – they are a perversion. Meditation on 1 John 4:16, ("God is love, and that they who dwell in love, dwell in God, and God in them.") led Hicks to offer the following as part of ministry delivered to Friends in Jericho Meeting during the War of 1812:

"All such among Christians who pray for the downfall or overcoming of their enemies by force of war – or by any other means than pure disinterested love – pray not in a Christian spirit, nor by the leading and influence of the Spirit of God, but in their own spirit, and by the leading and influence of the spirit of antichrist. Therefore, such prayers are not heard, but are an abomination in the sight of a pure and holy God, who cannot behold iniquity with approbation." (Journal, p. 228)

War Taxes are Corporate Sin

It is unlikely a prayer for victory would have been heard in a meeting for worship during the War of 1812, but that conflict confronted Friends with a choice still faced today: how to avoid supporting, even indirectly, the war. Unlike today, that war wasn't financed from general revenues – the undifferentiated income taxes, corporate taxes, and other sources of government income that fund twenty-first-century military adventures. Both state and national governments levied special taxes to wage war.

There was no way to pay them without acknowledging the use to which they would be put. Some Friends complied, while others refused to pay, preferring to suffer distrain - i.e., passively accepting the seizure of goods and property by the government in lieu of payment. Hicks recorded the disputes this provoked among Friends at a quarterly meeting in 1815:

> *"[There was] diversity of sentiment among the active members respecting... the active compliance in the payment of a tax... And for refusing the payment of thereof, a number of Friends had suffered in their property by distrain to a considerable amount more than the tax demanded - some even three or four-fold - whilst some others actively complied and paid the tax, and justified themselves in so doing, which caused considerable altercation in the meeting." (Journal, p. 225)*

For Hicks, this was not just a matter of procedure - the government got its money either way - but of corporate sin. One might even argue that, since the value of the distraint was often much more than the taxes owed, willing compliance would minimize the amount used to wage war. But paying the taxes implicitly sanctioned the war; and anyone who paid them deserved a share of responsibility for the war and all its consequences.

> *"I felt my mind deeply engaged to lay before Friends the inconsistency of our actively complying with any such military requisitions - believing that if we did, we should not only become accessories in the war, but should have to bear a part of the guilt of shedding the blood of our fellow creatures." (Journal, p. 175)*

Quakers who voluntarily paid war taxes were "pulling down with one hand what we are pretending to build with the other." (*Journal*, p. 344)

Challenges

Living in the World

The members and attenders of twenty-first-century Friends Churches and Meetings are, by and large, active in politics and government affairs. They vote. They work in political campaigns. Some even hold government office. The descendants of nineteenth-century Hicksites tend to be politically liberal and might hope Elias Hicks would be proud of their work. I believe Hicks would find they have too readily accepted the unacceptable, a degree of involvement - indeed of utter entanglement - in the world. I believe he would not be persuaded that contemporary Friends manage to be "*in* the world, but not *of* it."

Hicks' critiques of business and government still merit reflection. The specific career path he recommended to Samuel Evans – to work in "some mechanical branch" – may no longer be realistic for large numbers of people, but do we seek a "manner of life [that] is generally conducive to health, and freer from care and less burdensome to the mind"? More to his point, do we seek employment "which will much less interfere with our religious duty and conduce more to the general good of Society"? And by "Society," Hicks meant the Religious Society of Friends.

The American government has repeatedly demonstrated its willingness to use lethal force to achieve its goals – even sending drones to fire missiles at its own people. As citizens, most Quakers vote and, by voting, we legitimize the resulting government (whether we voted for the winners or the losers) and we unavoidably earn and deserve a share of the guilt for the violence and coercion done in our names.

When we vote, are we doing God's will?

Do we knowingly and willingly "bear a part of the guilt of shedding the blood of our fellow creatures"?

Slavery

"To rob a rational being of his liberty and free agency is to rob him of every thing valuable in this world that he could possibly possess or enjoy."
(Letters, p. 13)

Besides family and religion, there was nothing that aroused Elias Hicks' passion more than the absolute necessity to utterly eradicate slavery and to acknowledge the full humanity of "the Africans and their descendants." Half-measures were intolerable - he would accept nothing less than immediate emancipation with full compensation for the lives stolen and sufficient training to allow the freed men and women to support themselves and their families with dignity.

When the British Parliament passed "An Act for the Abolition of the Slave Trade" in 1807, it was hailed as the greatest humanitarian measure ever enacted and Thomas Clarkson was heaped with praise for his relentless lobbying on its behalf. In reaction - as much to the praise as to the act itself - Hicks wrote a bitterly scathing essay, *Lamentation and Weeping and Great Mourning* (*Letters*, pp. 11-16). In it, he excoriated the Parliament and all those who celebrated passage of the act because it only outlawed the slave trade, not slavery itself. Even more horrifying, the act recognized the rights of slave owners - rights that previously had not been written in British law. He asked Englishmen to consider how they would feel about the act if it applied to Bristol instead of the African coast. If white Englishmen had been robbed, kidnapped from their homes, and sold into slavery, would it be sufficient to forbid the transportation of newly enslaved people without freeing those already in bondage? The final paragraph of the essay is:

"The forgoing essay is addressed to the consideration of Thomas Clarkson with the rest of the Negroes' friends in Great Britain, hoping that, inasmuch as they have been favored through much labor and toil so far to prevail with the legislative body of their country as to make an attempt to compel their subjects to cease from robbery and murder – which is no act of

justice, at least to those they have already robbed and murdered – they may not give over the struggle until they prevail with them to do justice by restoring to the injured and deeply oppressed Africans, and their descendants that are held in slavery in their colonies, their just rights and equal liberties. And that full restitution be made them for all their false imprisonment and cruel oppressions." (Letters, p. 16)

As a measure of the depth of his abhorrence of slavery, Hicks was willing to violate his otherwise absolute rejection of any Quaker involvement in the political process. In seeking abolition (and for abolition only) he actively advocated petitioning the government and worked to get formal statements from Friends Meetings.

By 1816, most, but not all, of the enslaved population in New York had been freed. That year, he appealed to the Meeting for Sufferings (an executive committee for the body) of New York Yearly Meeting to act. In his memoirs, he calmly described the action taken by that body:

"In the course of the business that came before us, the meeting was led into an exercise on behalf of that portion of the descendants of the Africans that are still held in bondage in our state, and a proposition was made for addressing our state legislature on their accounts, in order if possible, to obtain a law for their emancipation... After due consideration, the proposition was acceded to and a committee named to draft an essay of an address accordingly." (Journal, p. 283)

Hicks may have been an unbending moral absolutist in nearly every other respect, but to gain freedom and justice for enslaved African-Americans, he was willing to (sometimes) temper his words and even make a deal with the devil.

The Spiritual Costs of Slaveholding

Like John Woolman, the famous Quaker abolitionist of the eighteenth century, Hicks realized enslavement damaged the souls of both those who were deprived of their freedom and those who unjustly held them. Being a slave owner erodes a person's humanity, but even more, Hicks saw the burdens and costs inflicted on the children of slaveholders.

Woolman was noted for approaching slave masters with love and compassion. Elias Hicks could be compassionate and forgiving, but most often he took a different tack – throwing cold light on the wickedness of what they were doing and on its evil consequences. In 1797, while visiting Indian Spring Friends Meeting in Maryland – an area with a substantial enslaved population – Hicks attended a meeting for worship at which non-Quaker slave owners were present. In the course of the meeting, he felt a divine imperative to offer the following ministry – to good effect:

> *"I was led in a plain, full, and clear manner to expose the enormous sin of oppression and of holding our fellow creatures in bondage, with the pernicious fruits and effects of it to those who are guilty thereof – and especially to their children who, being supported by the labor and toil of those held in slavery and thereby brought up in idleness, were led into pride and a very false and dark idea respecting God and his superintending providence, and many other evils fatal to their present and eternal well being, and tending to disqualify them from being useful in almost any respect, either to themselves or society, and thereby rendered unworthy of the respect of wise and good men, and therefore, are pests in society until reformed from those practices…*
>
> *"Since which, I have been informed that a woman present at that season, who possessed a number of slaves, was so fully convinced as to set them free, and joined in membership with Friends not long after." (Journal, p. 74)*

Slave Goods

The Quaker testimonies against war and slavery were intimately intertwined. It was common practice for countries at war to seize goods belonging to their enemies and sell them, with the profits helping to pay the costs of the war. Commercial ships captured at sea were a rich source of such "prize goods." Often these products would be offered for sale at prices considerably below their market value. As part of their testimony against war, Quakers refused to deal in prize goods.

Historically, prisoners of war were also considered prize goods and frequently enslaved. The slave trade provided an incentive for Africans to wage war against their neighbors for the sole purpose of taking prisoners - prize goods to be sold in the Americas.

Some Friends came to see any products produced directly or indirectly by slave labor as prize goods and, therefore, off-limits. For a brief time in the early years of the nineteenth century, some American yearly meetings adopted this position and called on their members to boycott such products, but they soon backed away. Influential Quakers who were involved in commerce argued the nineteenth-century international economy was so completely integrated that it was nearly impossible to distinguish slave goods and those tainted by slavery from those produced exclusively by free labor – a very modern rationalization. Hicks rejected it – that a thing is difficult does not excuse unfaithfulness.

Many of the ships that carried captives to the slave markets and transported slave goods in the trade that supported the slave system operated out of Providence, Rhode Island. There was a relatively large and prosperous Quaker community in the state and, in previous centuries, Quakers had owned and mastered slave ships. When the Religious Society of Friends testified against slavery, most of these Friends abandoned direct involvement in the slave trade, but they and their successors still profited from transshipping slave goods, such as rum and sugar from the West Indies and cotton from the American South. In 1816, Hicks challenged a meeting in Providence:

> *"The serpentine wisdom [that] works to the deceiving [of] multitudes was brought to light and exposed – especially that cunning, sophistical reasoning in the wisdom of this world that many people are making use of to justify themselves, and thereby stifle and put to silence the convictions of conscience, while acting in direct opposition to this pure principle of justice by continuing a traffic in and making themselves rich by a commerce in the produce of the labor of the poor, afflicted, and deeply oppressed Africans and their descendants held in a state of slavery by the mere force of war, and which is wrested from them by its cruel force without their consent. Truth was exalted over all, and unrighteousness exposed, and its evil effects on societies and individuals manifested." (Journal, p. 264)*

Hicks advocated a boycott of all slave goods and goods tainted by slavery. Beyond their status as prize goods, he understood that money undergirded the whole slave system. Without the income gained from the sale of these products, slavery would not be profitable. If enough people refused to buy slave goods, he reasoned, the whole system would collapse.

Purchasing Freedom

In general, Elias Hicks was rigid and uncompromising in his judgments and he certainly believed the slaveholders had no right to receive any compensation. Indeed, he felt they should be made to bear the financial burdens associated with manumission – paying reparations for the years of life and labor stolen, and providing the training or education needed to equip freed women and men with the skills to support themselves and their families. Nevertheless, he was pragmatic enough to consider purchasing and emancipating slaves.

He saw how much money was donated for such activities as missionary work, distributing Bibles, and supporting Christian Greeks in their war for independence from Muslim Turks. Would it not have been better, he wondered, to spend that money on manumission? In an essay, *Observations and Remarks on the Present State of Christendom* (*Letters*, pp. 193-96), he commented:

> *"Had the people of Great Britain and the United States applied the funds they have collected for the use of Bible and Missionary Societies... for the benefit of their poor slaves, how many ten thousand it would have relieved from their cruel bondage! ...*
>
> *"[And] instead of being led away by the popular delusion to help the Greeks, turned their attention home to the oppressed in our own land and about our own doors – poor innocent victims whom we have reduced by the most wanton cruelty to a state ten-fold more wretched and oppressive than has ever fallen to the lot of the Greeks – and had entered into associations to have done justice to those whom we had wantonly robbed and spoiled, how much more acceptable would it have been in the eyes of him who is perfect in justice and equity...*
>
> *"And had they taken the same pains to have collected funds for the just and noble purpose above-said – to have effected the emancipation and settlement of the people of color in our land to whom we are deeply indebted." (Letters, p. 195)*

Continuing in the essay, he addressed the need for newly-freed people to have safe places to live. Like many others of his time, Hicks did not believe the freed women and men would be permitted to exercise their full rights in lands dominated by whites, so he looked to what was then the newly opened lands (although it must be acknowledged, they were newly stolen from the Native Americans) in Alabama, Mississippi, Arkansas, and Louisiana as a possible homeland in which they might enjoy true freedom.

> *"I have no doubt but a sufficient sum would soon be collected to emancipate all the slaves in our country and procure a place of settlement for them in the southwestern interior of the United States where they might be assisted to settle a state or colony by themselves." (Letters, pp. 195-96)*

The Special Role of Friends

Although his initial objective may have simply been emancipation, as the years went by, he realized merely freeing a woman or man was not sufficient. Enslaved and free African-Americans suffered alike from widespread and deeply engrained racial bigotry. During an 1818 business meeting in Jericho, he called on Friends to lead the way in securing recognition of their full humanity and equality.

> *"It fell to my lot in the meeting for discipline to revive the concern for the melioration of the condition of the Africans and their descendants – not only as it respected those who are still held in a state of abject bondage and oppression, but also on behalf of those who have been set free, but who, nevertheless continue (in a very general manner) in a degraded and helpless state for want of being placed… upon the ground of equality with the rest of the inhabitants. And I am fully in the belief that divine justice will not be satisfied, nor the black stain for the shedding of innocent blood and cruelly oppressing of this people will ever be taken from the inhabitants of this land until that strict justice is done them and they placed by the laws of our country in the same state of equality – in every respect – as the rest of its inhabitants… [which] would bring them to be as good and useful citizens as those of any other nation.*
>
> *"I also was led to call upon my Friends to persevere in this noble and righteous concern… not only on their account and for their relief, but that on our own accounts also, as believing we are in a very peculiar manner called upon… And believing, as I do, that it is not in the power and wisdom of man to effect this by all coercive laws that can be enacted, nor by all the force of the arm of flesh… Hence, I believe that if we as a people were faithful and obedient to this first principle of our profession, we should be led thereby to abstain from all kinds of commerce or dealings in the produce of our country (or elsewhere) that we had good cause to believe originated out of or through the medium of the labor of slaves… [and] put a full end to oppression and injustice. And I believe he who called our worthy predecessors to exalt the testimony of Truth in the earth, and who is still calling us to advocate this noble cause, is looking for this testimony of strict justice and righteousness at our hands." (Journal, pp. 336-37)*

Government action, coercion, and violence are all inadequate and unreliable. Real change requires the transformation of people's hearts. Quakers need to be a clear example of such change. The Society of Friends needs to live up to its divine calling and be a light unto the nations.

Things I Believe But Can't Prove

To my knowledge, Elias Hicks never directly addressed the question of helping people who had escaped from slavery. Organized activities such as the Underground Railroad were still in development when he died and he may not have had any contact with them - although his daughter, Abigail, and her husband, Valentine Hicks, were participants in later years. Their home, just across the street from his in Jericho, sheltered fugitives. It would certainly have been consistent with his character to have assisted those seeking freedom and I doubt he would have had any qualms about breaking the relevant human laws. The divine law written in his heart and on his mind would have compelled him to do so.

Unlike many early nineteenth-century Friends, Hicks rejected all "gradualist" plans for abolition. Had he lived only a few years longer, I believe he would have endorsed the "moral suasion" tactics of non-violence and passive resistance advocated by William Lloyd Garrison and the New England Anti-Slavery Society in the 1830s.

John Brown's raid on Harpers Ferry and the Civil War were still three decades in the future when he died. There are hints in his writings that he accepted the principle that violence begets violence and I suspect he would have opposed any use of armed force to end slavery.

Even so, I believe he would have been tender toward those Quaker men who volunteered to serve in the Union army. Slavery was a supreme evil. It was the one thing for which he was willing to bend his principles. I can't believe he would have condemned those whose consciences compelled them to take up arms against it.

Challenges

There are more people enslaved in the world today than there ever were in the past. Millions of children are held in domestic servitude and millions of women have been forced into prostitution. Avoiding involvement with these particular activities is easy, but the modern slave system is more insidious. For example, much of the chocolate marketed in the world is made from cacao beans harvested by people who are effectively enslaved - and chocolate is not the only product tainted by contemporary slavery.

While it may not be simple to know if a particular product is tainted by slave labor, there are alternatives that are certified as “clean.” It just takes a little effort to seek them out.

Are we clear of modern prize goods?

The Great Separations

"O how unstable a creature is man! Full and empty, joyful and sorrowful, as things go well or ill. And all this is for want of having the mind centered in and on God, its alone proper object and sure balance of the soul."
(Journal, p. 240)

In 1827, a dispute within Philadelphia Yearly Meeting that had been simmering for years boiled over and the body split in two. The immediate cause of the separation was a disagreement over who would preside at that year's annual business meeting, but the underlying issues were theological, economic, and political. These were further aggravated by social and personality differences between the two groups and disputes over the proper exercise of authority in the Religious Society of Friends. Following the division, both subgroups claimed to be the true and rightful heirs of early Friends and the only faithful adherents to one hundred and seventy five years of Quaker tradition. Both also asserted proper possession of the titles "Friend" and "Quaker" and quickly took to referring to their opposite numbers as "the Orthodox" or "the Hicksites."

Both had legitimate claims to the tradition and the name.

This division was a uniquely defining event in the history of the Religious Society of Friends. Almost since its beginnings in the seventeenth century, there had been periodic disputes within the society that led to brief schisms. In each case, relatively small groups split off, maintained a separate existence for a time, and eventually either rejoined the main body or dissipated entirely. The Great Separations were different - both sides encompassed substantial populations and, despite repeated efforts which have achieved limited re-unifications in the years since, both have endured. More than that, this massive rupture in the society's unity fostered a cascade of further splits, separations, and splintering. It is no exaggeration to say all subsequent Quaker history was foreshadowed in the events of 1827-28.

An analysis of the Great Separations is beyond the scope of this book. There were several specific charges pressed against Elias Hicks and these have been highlighted in the chapters devoted to his beliefs. For those readers looking for an in-depth examination of the principal issues, the events leading up to the Great Separations, the major personalities involved, and the immediate aftermath of that break, the best available resource is Larry Ingle's *Quakers in Conflict*.[1]

Apostasy

For Hicks - as for many Friends in the 1820s - the separations were understood as merely the latest iteration of an ancient cycle in the history of humanity's relationship with the divine. Following the lead of early Friends and the leaders of the Protestant Reformation, they believed the theory of apostasy explained the course of that relationship.

In brief, this theory holds that God, out of love, periodically sent a prophet to call people to faithfulness. An ancient example is found in God's words in Jeremiah 7:23, "Obey my voice, and I will be your God, and ye shall be my people: and walk ye in all the ways that I have commanded you, that it may be well unto you." Almost invariably, the people's first response was a promise of fidelity, but the initial fervor burned off and gradually the people found less and less room in their lives for God. Other things became more important, crowding out the practice of their faith. This falling away from faithfulness defines apostasy. Over time, the divine-human relationship becomes increasingly estranged until, eventually, another prophet is dispatched and the cycle begins anew.

This process could be seen as essentially redundant, with each sequence of revival and apostasy leading back to the same conditions, but Hicks believed it spiraled upward - each reform was progressive, calling the people closer to God than they had ever been before, and each apostasy, a temporary falling back to an earlier stage. He read the Bible's Hebrew Testament as repeated iterations of this story. God sent prophets - Moses, Elijah, Isaiah, Jeremiah, and others - to call Israel to renewed faithfulness. But more than that, each prophet set a higher standard for devotion and fidelity than that of the messengers who came earlier - and each for a time succeeded.

---

[1] Ingle, H. Larry, *Quakers in Conflict: The Hicksite Reformation*. Wallingford, PA: Pendle Hill, 1998.

Jesus was sent to radically re-form humanity's relationship with God, doing away with outward rites and rituals and establishing a new inward covenant with God, but the early Christians, too, fell into apostasy. To Friends, this was demonstrated by the continued use of water baptism and other outward ordinances - old forms retained from the old covenant. These had been properly practiced under that covenant, but among Christians, these rituals became outward signs of their failure to live up to the new, spiritual covenant. Because of this renewed infidelity, the cycle of apostasy and reform had to continue through the work of new apostles like Francis of Assisi, Jan Huss, Martin Luther, and George Fox.

As Hicks read the record of repeated, failed reformations, each one had decayed as the first generation of reformers passed from the scene. Their successors lacked first-hand experience of God's powerful call to a new level of faith and faithfulness. The second generation didn't feel the passion that had animated the work of reform; so they were satisfied to simply maintain past gains - or even to abandon those gains and fall into apostasy. As the first generation died, so did the zeal that had propelled the reformation. He described this process in a letter to William Poole:

> *"It is sorrowful to observe that every right step of reformation has gone down to the grave with the first instruments of such reform or soon after. Their successors... have set down at ease in their labors – as though the work was now completed... The reformation through Moses and Joshua and the Elders of Israel lasted no longer than to the death of all these. And the several reforms after the death of these – by prophets and such as the Lord raised up for that end – were of short duration. So likewise, the reform produced by Jesus and his disciples lasted very little longer than to the life of John, the beloved apostle." (Letters, p. 179)*

William Penn wrote that once the slide into apostasy began, the natural sequence was for succeeding generations to seek worldly power to bolster their ecclesiastical status, wielding the magistrate's sword to enforce their religious authority[2]. Ironically, Penn's sons and grandsons chose to retain political power as Proprietors of Pennsylvania, but left the Religious Society of Friends.

In keeping with Penn's analysis, Hicks noted the successors to one set of reformers frequently sought to consolidate their authority by uniting

---

[2] See, for example, the preface to Penn's *The Christian Quaker* in Buckley, Paul (Ed.), *Twenty-First Century Penn.* Richmond, Indiana: Earlham School of Religion Publications, 2003, pp. 65-66.

church and state. The power of the state was then used to persecute the next wave of reformers.

"For each of those many varied sects of professed Christians (in their turn), as they got the power of the civil magistrates on their side, would endeavor – by the sword, by severe edicts, and banishment – to reduce and destroy all those who dissented from them, although their opinions were not a whit more friendly to real, genuine Christianity than the tenets of their opposers. For all were – in great measure, if not entirely – adulterated and apostatized from the true spirit of Christianity that breathes peace on earth and good will to man." (Journal, pp. 226-27)

Quaker Apostasy

It may be human nature to believe the current state of reform is the last and perfection has finally been achieved. Whenever that is the case, further reformation is not just unnecessary, it is wrong. With this mindset, the reformers or their successors naturally seek to consolidate the great gains they have inherited and to resist any attempts to change things further. Quakers, Hicks wrote to Poole, were not immune to this way of thinking:

"George Fox was raised up as a peculiar instrument in the Lord's hand to bear testimony to the primitive foundation – the Light or Spirit of Truth within – as the only true teacher and sure rule of faith and practice... But alas, what shall we say? Have not his successors, like the successors of the foregoing reformers, too much settled down in the labors of their predecessors and became too generally dry and formal? And instead of advancing the reformation, [Friends] are in danger of going back and not forward... And if this continues to be the case, shall we fare better than those who have gone before us? Or rather, ought we not to conclude – agreeable to former precedents – that the Lord ere long will raise up some one or more to bear testimony against this false peace and formal unity and break all the bands of unhallowed tradition, which make void the commands of God." (Letters, pp. 146-47)

Furthermore, Hicks believed, too many Friends had forsaken the unique treasure revealed to them – the universal availability of immediate spiritual guidance from the Inward Light – and were instead turning away and looking for direction from outward things, especially from the Bible. This, he described as paralleling the failure of the early Christians to ground the primitive church in that unshakable spiritual foundation.

"Had the successors of the apostles attended (as they ought to have done) to the command given by Jesus to his disciples to wait for the promise of the Holy Spirit… the apostasy never could have entered. But instead thereof, they turned their attention to the letter, one crying, 'I am of Paul,' another, 'I of Apollos,' etc., and neglected the spirit. Hence divisions and contentions originated in the church, and destroyed the peace and unity thereof, and in process of time plunged it into a desperate state of total darkness.

"The same fate – from the same cause – has befallen in a great degree our poor Society. But had Friends kept to the Light and Spirit of Truth… no apostasy could have entered, but the Society ere now would have made great advancements on the labors and experience of those early worthies. Many things would have opened in succession on the minds of the faithful, by the same Light of Truth that George Fox and the people of that day could not have borne. But instead thereof, Friends turning their attention back to the letter of the Scriptures and the writings of our primitive Friends… have blocked up their own way by an undue attention to the letter." (Letters, pp. 184-85)

Elias Hicks & the Separations

Hicks never explicitly claimed to have been "raised up to bear testimony against a false peace," but clearly he saw himself as part of a new round of reform. When he was accused of unsoundness, he may well have taken the charge as an endorsement - when apostasy is ascendant, the truly faithful are called unsound. When a neighbor denounced him and accused him of being alone in his views, Hicks wrote back:

"For thy sentiments and manner of reasoning entirely shuts up the way of reform, and by which thou condemns every reformer that God in his wisdom and mercy has called by his grace to go forth single-handed to protest against the deadness, formality, and superstition of the church or society they were associated with. [For] instance, Luther, Calvin, Fox, and in latter days, Woolman, Benezet, etc… For it never has been manifest in the records of any church I have had the perusal of, that there ever were ten of its members united together in the first beginning of a reformation. And my memory doesn't serve me with a single instance where any more than one individual has been called to set about the work of reform at its first beginning… the strength of individuals does not consist in numbers and therefore, if I stood alone – as Fox and Woolman did in the beginning of

their day – it would have no effect at all to make me turn aside or shrink from what I esteemed my duty, for I am not accountable to man in matters of conscience. So I also know in whom I have believed, and in whom is all my trust and confidence placed for support and preservation." (Letters, pp. 155-56)

Whether he considered himself a prophet or not, he often spoke as one. As early as 1813, while visiting in several Friends Meetings in Philadelphia Yearly Meeting, he was moved to call for revival:

"I was led forth generally in those meetings in close, searching testimonies, tending to arouse Friends from their beds of ease and carnal security – brought upon them by an inordinate love of the world and an increase of temporal blessings, in which their principal enjoyments were too much centered – loving the gifts and forgetting the giver." (Journal, p. 153)

Nor did he only challenge "ordinary" Quakers. In 1817, he was back in Philadelphia - this time participating in the Meeting of Ministers and Elders. The Friends present held positions of authority in the pre-eminent yearly meeting in North America; they were accustomed to receiving deference from other Friends. The Ministers and Elders probably did not welcome a lecture.

"On Third Day, the quarterly meeting opened there with a Meeting of Ministers and Elders, in which I was led to open to Friends of that meeting the great obligations and accountability that attached to those who consented to take seats in such meetings, which placed us in the forefront of society and consequently were looked to as the leaders of the people. And therefore, if we should fall short in faithfully holding up those precious testimonies we are called to bear for the Prince of Peace, and in leading forward the flock by advancing the reformation as Truth opens the way, we shall become stumbling-blocks in the way of the honest travelers, and thereby shut up their way to improvement – by which they may be discouraged and fall back and be lost. In consequence whereof (it is to be feared), their blood might be required at the hands of such unfaithful and dilatory shepherds." (Journal, pp. 315-16)

Elias Hicks never sought the leadership of a reform movement, but as perhaps the best known American Quaker minister of his day, he was inevitably drawn into the conflicts leading up to the Great Separations. He had traveled widely and often, throughout much of English-speaking North America. In meetings with other Friends, he spoke out forcefully - even harshly - in advocating what he considered to be traditional

Quakerism. Because he frequently held public meetings, his words were heard not only by Quakers, but by thousands of outsiders. For those within the Quaker fold who disagreed with him, he was a public embarrassment.

Although he was in the thick of the disputes, Hicks did not write much about the events leading up to the separations. In two very short letters, he directly addressed what he considered to be unfair attacks. The first was to Caleb Pierce and others in response to an accusation of unsoundness (*Letters*, pp. 138-39). He rejected the charges outright, but without providing much information about their content or detailing his refutation of them. In the letter, Hicks was more concerned with who was empowered to judge him than with what he was to be judged about. According to "the right order of discipline," the complaints should have been filed with his home meeting in Jericho, New York, where he (and his opponents) knew they would be dismissed.

The second letter was to Anna Braithwaite, an evangelical Friend from England who twice visited with Hicks at his home. Contrary to accepted Friends' practice, she published an account of her conversation with him without seeking permission from the yearly meeting or informing Hicks she was planning to do so. Hicks' recollection of the event was very different from hers, but again, he claimed to be most concerned about her violations of the discipline. In his letter, he said he forgave her, but could have no more communication with her "until thou makes a suitable acknowledgment for thy breach of friendship and the salutary discipline of our society" (*Letters*, p. 197). As with the letter to Caleb Pierce, this one was very brief and provides very little information.

Following the separations in Philadelphia and New York Yearly Meetings, Hicks felt called to undertake the longest ministerial journey of his life. This trip, which is described in vivid detail in his journal, included numerous confrontations with Orthodox Friends. In several, the Orthodox had taken possession of a meetinghouse and barred Hicksites from entering - locking doors and windows, sometimes even posting guards at the entries. In most cases, this was only a temporary nuisance, but on occasion, it led to physical confrontation between gangs of Hicksites and Orthodox. Friends even summoned the authorities to have other Friends arrested for trespassing in their own meetinghouse.

Being obstructed physically was an inconvenience. It hurt when his membership in the Religious Society of Friends was challenged. One instance occurred during the meeting for worship preceding the business meeting of New Garden Quarterly Meeting in Ohio:

> *"The members of that meeting had not fully separated, therefore they all assembled together – both Orthodox and Friends – although the Orthodox in their monthly meetings had disowned, in their presumptuous way, many of their brethren and sisters... And after a time of silence, I arose and addressed the meeting and Truth was raised into dominion.*
>
> *"But soon after I sat down, Thomas [Shillitoe, an English evangelical Friend] arose and warned the people not to be led away by me, that I was not a regular member of Society, that all the sound members of the quarterly and monthly meeting had testified against me, and seven yearly meetings out of eight had declared their disunity with me, and much more to the same import. And when he sat down, Jesse [Merritt, Hicks' traveling companion] informed the meeting that he was a member of the same monthly meeting that I was and he knew that what the Friend had declared was incorrect and contrary to truth. After which, I felt the way open to give a correct statement of matters relating to the subject, which appeared to give satisfaction to all present – except to Thomas and a few of his Orthodox adherents. And the people appeared greatly disgusted at his conduct, assuring one another in their conversation that the old Englishman was mad. And truly, he manifested great irritability and passion, both in words and gesture." (Letters, pp. 232-33)*

Notice Hicks spoke twice during worship – a minor violation of Friends' practice. In addition, Hicks, Thomas Shillitoe, and Jesse Merritt were engaged in an argument during worship – a more grievous violation of "the right order of Friends." Adding to this misconduct, all seem to have "manifested great irritability and passion" in the midst of what was intended to be a period of worship.

Things did not improve when the New Garden business sessions began. Only members of the society were supposed to attend business meetings. His credentials as a Public Friend (a minister authorized in writing by her or his home meeting to travel among Friends) and therefore as someone with the right to attend were again challenged:

> *"Friends then called on such Public Friends that were strangers to produce their certificates. We then handed ours forward and they were read, but the Orthodox kept up their noise and clamor, ordering those who had no right to sit in the meeting to withdraw, but Friends paid no attention thereto,*

but urged the clerk to go on with the business, which he did whenever he could be heard." (Letters, p. 233)

Back on Long Island, two small, dissident factions withdrew from the Monthly Meetings in Jericho and Westbury, New York, and combined to form a new Orthodox monthly meeting. They claimed to be the only true Friends left in the area and proceeded to disown everyone else – the overwhelming majorities in each of their original meetings. But first, they sent a letter west to Ohio, ordering Hicks to return home. This demand seems to have affected a deeper hurt than anything else he encountered on the journey. In one of his few displays of obvious anger, he wrote home:

"Yesterday, five or six of the Orthodox ministers and elders waited on me with a communication from the new upstart Monthly Meeting of Jericho and Westbury... and informed me that the monthly meeting had agreed to order me to return immediately home and not to proceed any further in my proposed visit – and a copy of which they have likewise sent to the ministers and elders at this place, in order for them to stop me and send me home... I think our monthly meeting ought to make out a correct statement of their proceedings as a remonstrance against them and send it on to me signed by the clerk and a double number of our members to the whole number of the Orthodox who constituted the new upstart monthly meeting... thirteen in number. Now, if a correct remonstrance was made out and signed by the clerk and thirty or more of our members, and I could get it published here (which would be readily done), it would be a very great strength and comfort to Friends here and greatly promote our cause among the people and liberate me from their numerous untrue accusations." (Letters, pp. 238-39)

Two weeks later, he had received a letter of endorsement from Jericho Meeting but was not satisfied with it. The denunciations were not strong enough, and the meetings had not been punitive enough.

"And although I received a certificate yesterday signed by a number of Friends, yet it fell short of giving a full and correct statement, for it ought fully to have set forth how that there was no such monthly meeting acknowledged under the title of the Monthly Meeting of Westbury and Jericho in the Yearly Meeting of New York, and setting forth the names of the persons who... had separated themselves from the body of Friends and set up a little separate meeting... And I am fully persuaded that if the Monthly Meetings of Westbury and Jericho rightly consider the matter, they will feel it to be their incumbent duty to treat with and disown all

those members who have thus risen up against the Truth and trampled upon the right order and discipline of the Society." (Letters, p. 242)

Three weeks later, he was still stewing. In a letter to his son-in-law, Valentine Hicks, he ranted that the members of "the little upstart" meeting must have "fallen into a state of mental derangement." (*Letters*, p. 244)

In due course, the Orthodox meeting disowned him, but by then, he seems to have concluded they were of little consequence:

"I received a copy of my testification and disownment from the Orthodox yesterday week. And it contains two and a half columns of paper as large as this and is a short history – mostly of lies and falsehoods." (Letters, p. 262)

Hicksites

It is no accident one of the two sets of meetings emerging from the separations was labeled Hicksite. Like so many other names (including "Quaker"), this title was initially intended to disparage, not to praise. Orthodox Friends applied it to their opponents to indicate that those former compatriots were not real Friends – no longer members of the religious movement started by George Fox, but followers of a new and false prophet, Elias Hicks. As with "Quaker," the name stuck and was eventually embraced by his friends. Some Friends today still proudly call themselves Hicksites.

Although the term, "Hicksite" was in use during his lifetime, Elias Hicks did not acknowledge it in his correspondence. He expressed his preference for the term "Tolerants," or simply wrote of "real Quakers" when distinguishing them from "the Orthos."

Things I Believe But Can't Prove

Elias Hicks was eighty years old when the separations propagated through the yearly meetings of North America. He remained active among Friends – continuing to travel and writing a steady stream of letters – but took no formal role in the emerging Hicksite meetings.

There is no hint of regret for the splits that took place. Despite his calls for tolerance and repeated claims he bore no animus toward his opponents, he seemed glad to see them gone. In fact, I believe his personal feelings regarding some in the leadership of Philadelphia Yearly Meeting (and their reciprocal rancor) widened the impending breach in the 1820s and made it increasingly difficult to avoid the eventual separation.

Many of the central actors on both sides of the separations were quite simply, grumpy old white men who didn't much like each other. Hicks' opponents treated him with little respect - in one instance, adjourning a business meeting while he was out of the room as a snub. He clearly felt they misrepresented his theological views. In return, Hicks denied their authority - rejecting their attempts to exercise what they saw as proper discipline within their yearly meeting. Neither side showed any enthusiasm for efforts to mediate their differences.

By 1827, both sides were convinced "we are right and you are wrong." This made the differences irreconcilable and divorce inevitable.

Rather than a tragedy, Elias Hicks believed he was witnessing the beginnings a new reformation, one that would result in a new level of faithfulness among Friends - at least within the faithful remnant that represented the true Religious Society of Friends.

So did his opponents.

Coming Home

The day following rode to my own home and (with a mind full of peace and solid satisfaction – the sure reward of obedience) found my dear wife and children all well. And with open, cordial, and sympathetic affection, embraced each other in endeared and mutual love. For which favor, as also for the manifold, unmerited mercies and preservations I have from time to time received, my spirit bows in humble adoration before thee, O Lord God of our health and salvation, and desires to ascribe unto thee greatness with glory, thanksgiving, and high renown, for thou art worthy to receive it throughout all ages and generations, world without end. Amen.
(Journal, p. 44)

One More Thing I Believe But Can't Prove

It is a clear, crisp Long Island afternoon. The sun sits low in the pale blue sky. Last night's dusting of snow has sifted into the brittle grass.

Halfway between the house and barn, a couple is embraced. His head is bent to hers; the broad brim of his hat tents them, hiding their faces.

In the kitchen, Elisabeth is pulling together a simple supper. She has sent Abigail and Valentine's son back across the narrow road to fetch his parents, and then on around the corner, to alert Aunt Martha and Uncle Royal Aldrich.

It will be some minutes more before the traveler unclasps to greet his children and grandchildren.

Appendix: Quaker Structure, Practice & Terminology

Structure

In the eighteenth and nineteenth centuries, the Religious Society of Friends was organized in a hierarchical structure. Individuals would attend meeting for worship at a local congregation called a **preparative meeting** (because it prepared items for business meetings). Several preparative meetings would gather together each month to conduct business as a **monthly meeting**. Representatives from the monthly meetings in an area assembled every three months (or quarterly) to conduct business as a **quarterly meeting**. Likewise, there was an annual business meeting for the representatives from a somewhat wider geographical area to conduct business as a **yearly meeting**.

Although there were several yearly meetings, there was no single unifying body to govern the whole - even before the Great Separations. London Yearly Meeting was generally viewed as first among equals and, within the United States, Philadelphia Yearly Meeting was similarly seen as having more weight than the other yearly meetings.

It was felt women would not be able to exercise the authority needed to conduct their business if men were present, so there were separate business meetings for men and women at each level.

Worship

Meeting for worship was a service conducted in the traditional manner of Friends. At this time, all Friends worship services were unprogrammed, that is, without a preplanned order of service and with no worship leader.

At a designated time, the congregation would gather in silence in an unadorned meeting room. If one or more members felt called by God to preach, she or he would do so. Sometimes, a meeting would pass without any spoken ministry. It was assumed anyone present could be divinely inspired to speak. Although women and men sat on separate sides of the meetinghouse, there was no barrier between them during worship and any ministry offered was heard by all. Meeting for worship concluded when two ministers shook hands.

Offices

Quaker meetings had no paid or professional staff. The **Clerk** was a member appointed for a term to preside at business meetings. In principle, this conferred no special status on the individual asked to serve, but in practice, clerks exercised a great deal of influence in most meetings. Particularly skilled clerks often held the position for many years, even for decades.

Any man or woman who regularly offered valuable vocal ministry during meeting for worship might be recognized as a **Minister**. Ministers did not attend seminaries nor were they ordained. If the ministers and elders in a local meeting felt an individual had a gift for preaching, that person's name would be brought to a meeting of all the ministers and elders within the quarterly meeting. If that group concurred with the recommendation, the designation of minister was formally minuted by the monthly meeting.

Monthly meetings similarly named men and women to the station of **Elder.** The Elders shared responsibility for the spiritual condition of the meeting. This included nurturing (but not delivering) ministry during meeting for worship and fostering the spiritual growth of meeting members - especially of young people and ministers. The process by which Elders were called was similar to that for ministers.

Appointment as a minister or an elder was for life. An individual could not serve as both a minister and an elder.

In eighteenth and nineteenth century Quaker meetinghouses, there were two or three rows of "facing benches" at the front of the meeting room. Ministers and elders (including those visiting from other meetings) were expected to sit in those benches. The rest of the congregation sat in benches facing them.

This arrangement had practical value. Frequently, a "sounding board" was erected behind the facing benches to amplify the ministers' voices when they preached. In addition, the facing benches were raised, putting the elders in a position to easily see the whole congregation.

While the Elders were responsible for the spiritual condition of the meeting, the **Overseers** were concerned with temporal behavior. It was the overseers' duty to intervene with wayward members before their behavior required public discipline by the meeting. A successful intervention avoided embarrassment for both the member and the society. Overseers did not sit on the facing benches.

Traveling in the Ministry

The two most important things stitching the Religious Society of Friends together in the nineteenth century were epistles and traveling ministers.

Epistles were letters written by a yearly meeting and sent to other meetings. These included annual epistles, conveying greetings from one yearly meeting to the other yearly meetings, and epistles of instruction sent to subordinate meetings.

Traveling Ministers arose from the other end of the hierarchy. All Friends were, of course, free to visit other meetings, but to travel in the capacity of a recognized minister required permission from the individual's monthly meeting. This authorization included recognition the minister was a proper public face for the religious society, an endorsement of the proposed journey, and acceptance by the meeting of a responsibility to look after the traveler's family and temporal affairs while he or she was away. For travel beyond the bounds of one's own yearly meeting, approvals from both the minister's monthly meeting and quarterly meeting were required. An elder was named to accompany the minister.

The clerk of the meeting documented approval with a signed **Certificate** that the traveler carried during the journey. This document was presented to each meeting visited. Besides declaring the visitor's status, it conferred the right to attend local meetings of ministers and elders. The clerks of meetings visited would acknowledge the visit by writing a brief endorsement on the certificate. When the traveler's journey was completed, the certificate was returned to her or his home meeting.

A visit could be for a single day or the traveling minister might stay long enough to call at the home of each of the families in the meeting. Often he or she would "seek an opportunity" with the family.

Selected Quaker Terms

Appointed meeting: A meeting for worship not held at the usual times (i.e., Sunday morning, Sunday evening, or on a midweek evening). These were often public meetings - specifically inviting non-Quakers to attend - scheduled on behalf of a traveling minister. Meetings were held in a variety of locations, including meetinghouses, private homes, taverns, public buildings, and even outdoors.

Baptism: For Friends, baptism was an inward, spiritual event - the baptism "with the Holy Ghost and with fire" mentioned in the gospels (Matthew 3:11 and Luke 3:16). It was not something that occurred once in a lifetime; baptisms were repeated tests an individual endured as part of the lifelong process of salvation.

Day of Visitation: This was an important concept for early Friends, drawing on several scriptural references (e.g., Isaiah 10:3, Jeremiah 46:21 and 50:27, Hosea 9:7, Micah 7:4, and 1 Peter 2:12). Although the term was sometimes used to refer to the last judgment at the end of the world, it more often specified a time of trial in each person's life. During this time of visitation, he or she would be required to choose between faithfulness and salvation or self-gratification and eternal damnation. Some early Friends believed this was a single once-and-for-all event - if the wrong choice was made, the chance of salvation was lost forever. Hicks, however, believed God offered repeated opportunities for redemption.

Discipline: The standard for acceptable conduct among Friends.

Minute: The formal statement of a decision made in the course of a Quaker business meeting. When a decision was approved, it was "minuted" in a bound minute book.

Opportunity: An impromptu period of prayer and contemplation. These frequently occurred in Quaker homes when traveling ministers visited.

CPSIA information can be obtained
at www.ICGtesting.com
Printed in the USA
FSOW01n0546190615
8088FS